Praise for This Book

"Future readiness is a vital capability for talent development leaders. In *Forward-Focused Learning*, world-class TD execs describe the award-winning best practices that have prepared their organizations for what's next. This is a must-read to help you take your organization to the next level."

TONY BINGHAM
President and CEO, ATD

"*Forward-Focused Learning* goes well beyond L&D theory. It is a collection of lessons and real-life stories on application in some of today's leading organizations. A must read for any practitioner who is looking to refresh their toolkit."

TARA DEAKIN
Chief People Officer, Spin Master

"*Forward-Focused Learning* is a crash course in how to think like the world's best CLOs. From the contributors to the content, this book delivers cover to cover."

ANDRÉ MARTIN
VP and CLO, Google

FORWARD-FOCUSED LEARNING

INSIDE AWARD-WINNING ORGANIZATIONS

Edited by
TAMAR ELKELES

Foreword by
KIMO KIPPEN

ATD Press is an internationally renowned source of insightful and practical information on talent development, training, and professional development.

ATD Press
1640 King Street
Alexandria, VA 22314 USA

Ordering information: Books published by ATD Press can be purchased by visiting ATD's website at td.org/books or by calling 800.628.2783 or 703.683.8100.

Library of Congress Control Number: 2020943712
ISBN-10: 1-95049-667-8
ISBN-13: 978-1-95049-667-9
e-ISBN: 978-1-95049-668-6

ATD Press Editorial Staff
Director: Sarah Halgas
Manager: Melissa Jones
Content Manager: Ann Parker
Developmental Editor: Jack Harlow
Production Editor: Hannah Sternberg
Text Design: Shirley E.M. Raybuck
Interior Layout: Kathleen Dyson
Cover Design: Rose Richey

Printed by Versa Press, East Peoria, IL

Contents

Foreword: Welcome to the New Normal v
Kimo Kippen

Introduction ix
Tamar Elkeles

Chapter 1: Becoming a Strategic Business Driver. 1
Brad Samargya

Chapter 2: Designing an Effective Learning Organization 9
Susan Burnett

Chapter 3: Supercharging Your Learning Agenda Through
Purpose, Culture, and Brand 29
Andrew Kilshaw

Chapter 4: The Five Building Blocks of a Learning Ecosystem 41
Marina Theodotou

Chapter 5: Winning at Shark Tank: How L&D Leaders Really
Gain Management Support. 53
Kevin D. Wilde

Chapter 6: The Talent Behind an Award-Winning Learning Team 71
Gale Halsey

Chapter 7: Leaders as Teachers. 83
Jayne Johnson

Chapter 8: Do More With Less: Using Your Budget Wisely 95
Michelle Braden

Chapter 9: Impact Matters 107
Martha Soehren

Chapter 10: Collaborative Learning Drives Collective Ingenuity 119

Aimee George Leary, Ruth Almen, and Chris Holmes

Chapter 11: Agile Is the New Smart 131

Laura Lee Gentry and Annmarie Neal

Conclusion: Moving Forward 145

Tamar Elkeles

References 147

About the Contributors 149

Index 155

About the Editor 161

Foreword:
Welcome to the New Normal

Kimo Kippen

I call it the "new normal," this era of dynamic change we are experiencing and its profound impact on personal lives and businesses throughout the world. It began even before the COVID-19 epidemic descended on us all. But as I write this in the midst of that dreadful pandemic, its full impact will clearly be both global and seismic.

What will the future of this new normal look like? We don't know. But we do know it will require individuals and organizations alike to develop a dramatically heightened sense of resilience.

The challenge to meet this new standard begins with what I call a link back to purpose. Today's successful and forward-focused organizations are those that have defined their sense of purpose and how it links to their visions, missions, and values.

For learning and development organizations, both obligations and opportunities await. They will be on the front lines, after all, leading the way and ensuring that their organizations don't lapse into previous business practices. Fortunately, the talent development field is well positioned to meet these challenges, and indeed is already doing so by aggressively recognizing and pursuing new learning opportunities and delivery methods.

But I believe this new sense of resilience must begin on an individual level, with an increased sense of self-awareness, purpose, mission, vision, and values. It will then expand outwardly to family, to work, to teams, and to our social structures. Every aspect of our lives will have to be reframed in a way that starts with self. For many of us, that will require a complete reset on how we perceive and live our lives.

I know from personal experience that my own journey has always been centered around the concept of life's purpose. It has guided me at the personal, social, and workplace levels, and in the learning profession I care so deeply about. But for many others, this reset will be a more profound experience.

I also think people are hungry for that higher level of connection, commitment, and purpose, both personally and among organizations they relate to as members, employees, business partners, and customers. Like me, they believe their choices of where to spend time and money reflect their fundamental values and purpose in life. They believe that what they do matters, as do the organizations with which they relate.

That's why I'm gratified to have witnessed a resurgence in this link back to purpose, especially among organizations with which I have worked that define their missions and cultures for employees and customers alike. I am also proud that this sense of purpose has long been prioritized by the Association for Talent Development and its members worldwide.

ATD members are helping their organizations "crack the code" of this uncertain universe by creatively connecting vision, mission, and values to a greater sense of purpose. Indeed, the most useful and timely advice yet compiled to guide TD executives has already been articulated by some of the profession's most respected leaders. You are holding it in your hands!

Principal among their many insights is today's intense focus on the customer, and the impact of that focus on learning. It is where everything begins and ends for companies—or should be. Today, we are seeing in real time a dramatic change in the needs of customers. Yet there are silver linings to be found in times like these, both on personal and organizational levels.

The global population's universal need to go virtual during COVID-19—and the resulting impact on the hospitality industry and other fields—surely offers the most vivid example of impending change. I believe the experience will spur people to reset their personal priorities by dining out differently and taking vacations in a more solitary way. How will they do that while also sharing the experience with family and friends? Creative entrepreneurs will provide answers.

Talent development professionals are clearly at the center of this dynamic as they guide individuals and organizations through the shifting landscape of business, technology, and social awareness. Clearly, the new world for organizations will revolve around the customer more than ever. Companies that make the adjustment will see great opportunities.

Indeed, that adjustment has already begun. Examples include corporate decisions to elevate talent development to core competency status, regarded as vital to the bottom line as well as strategy and innovation. Companies suddenly view learning not as an HR-related function, but as the cornerstone of a customer-centric, agile business agenda.

TD departments have long been showing their organizations how to "go virtual," of course. Recent enhancements include the adoption of artificial intelligence and learner-friendly digital techniques borrowed from popular platforms such as Amazon Prime, Netflix, and YouTube. Convenient delivery platforms like Zoom and WebEx have ushered in a new era of high-touch and high-experience learning.

Meanwhile, TD departments are also helping their organizations adopt other forward-thinking methods such as design thinking, the bottom-up approach to creating innovation and challenging assumptions. L&D teams are embracing this iterative process to help build, nurture, and cultivate their own learning ecosystems while also molding new corporate cultures.

I believe the design thinking approach, often referred to as "slam teams" and many of them virtual, will become part of the DNA of successful organizations. But doing so will also require a different set of skills for leaders and a new mentality that embraces flexibility, open-mindedness, and group performance. Call it a core capability required for success within this new normal.

You will find these and many other practical insights included within these pages. I sincerely hope you will find them useful.

Introduction

Tamar Elkeles

"And the winner is . . ."

Across every profession, in every industry, the outstanding contributions and hard work of individuals, teams, and organizations are recognized as "the winners" or "the best." Sometimes there's the international spotlight of a World Series Championship, an Oscar, or the green jacket, and other times there's much less fanfare. Nonetheless, these significant award opportunities offer public validation for our efforts.

Recognition really does matter. Despite having nearly 30 years of professional work experience and having earned some very appreciated recognition throughout my career, I still remember winning my sixth-grade spelling bee, and I consider that one of the major highlights of my life. People often ask if I remember the winning word; unfortunately, I don't. What I do remember was the school-wide assembly and the feeling I had when my name was announced. I had my 15 minutes of fame. I was a winner.

From adolescence to adulthood in the workplace, we continue to seek recognition, not just for ourselves, but often for our teams. We instruct management in our organizations to consistently give meaningful performance feedback and rewards to employees for their exceptional performance. Top salesperson awards, employee of the month awards, top research awards—the list goes on. We are trained to give and receive recognition, no matter the stage of our life or the context.

Awards and Forward-Focused Learning

What does this mean to leaders in the talent development, organizational learning, and human capital industry? What do external recognition and awards—such as the ATD BEST and Excellence in Practice Awards, *Training* magazine's Training Top 100, and *CLO* magazine's Learning Elite and CLO of the Year—signify? Why pursue them? Notably, they serve to highlight and recognize the organizations that demonstrate award-winning and forward-focused learning.

The contributors in this book pride themselves on having created innovative and progressive approaches to developing talent in their organizations and improving both individual and organizational performance. They have worked tirelessly to develop and implement various learning initiatives, practices, and programs that have had a significant impact on their businesses. Their work became an essential part of their companies' employment brand and overall performance. Their companies are known as organizations where people can grow their careers and make important contributions to the company and its purpose. Having an award-winning learning organization demonstrates a company's commitment to employee growth and development.

These leaders have all helped to build great companies, and they represent individuals or organizations that have received external validation for their learning organization's successes and business impact.

Talent development professionals can learn a lot from award-winning organizations. Companies that are proactive about their learning and development—that always look for ways to grow, build, and learn—are highly deliberative in their process to implement new initiatives and leverage opportunities that enable growth. Their efforts result in their success and in achieving external award status. These organizations offer lessons not just for being the best or elite but also for being the most innovative, the most aligned to business needs, and the most strategic.

It's not often that we have the opportunity to peek behind the curtain and see how other companies and their leaders use learning to develop their employees and their businesses. That's the purpose of this book: to provide you with specific insights, perspectives, and strategies from CLOs, CHROs, and CTDOs across different industries and with unique executive experiences in forward-focused, award-winning learning organizations. This book invites you to learn from some of the most admired global learning leaders in the world about what it takes to be the best in our profession and within our industry. It is an honor to share these proven strategies and approaches about what it takes to be the best from these award-winning executives and their award-winning organizations.

Three broad themes are embodied in this book: vision, people, and process.

Vision

Leading a forward-focused learning organizations starts with vision. You cannot become a strategic business driver, design an effective learning organization, develop a compelling purpose and brand, or build a learning ecosystem without a vision for how to align with your company's core business goals and drivers.

Learning leaders need to step up and take responsibility for integrating learning into the business. This starts with building staff capability with a performance consultant mindset: Meeting with business leaders and speaking their language to set priorities, build successful learning plans, and eliminate talent gaps. Partnering with these leaders enables you to create strategic learning plans that have a direct impact on business performance. These plans become your best asset in demonstrating value and showcasing the link between your initiatives and business success. You can't let the conversation with business leaders occur only once a year—continuous conversation and communication ensures visibility and engagement.

Brad Samargya, former CLO at KPMG, in his chapter "Becoming a Strategic Business Driver," illustrates exemplary workforce development initiatives that deliver strategic business results. We often hear about the importance of aligning learning to the business, and in Brad's case, a learning organization doesn't have a strategic edge without it.

As Brad describes, business alignment doesn't happen overnight, and you can't take what's worked for one organization and apply it to your own. One size truly doesn't fit all—one size fits one. To design an effective and aligned learning organization, you need to ensure you have the right model in place. Transformation starts internally. It's essential to think systematically, and a helpful guide is Jay Galbraith's STAR model, which requires you to deeply understand the business strategy, and then examine the alignment or misalignment of the structures, processes, rewards, people, and culture that exist to execute that strategy. Conduct a current state assessment and then make a future state recommendation. The end result will be an aligned learning system that drives the larger business system.

Susan Burnett, former talent and learning executive at HP, Yahoo!, and Deloitte, in her chapter "Designing an Effective Learning Organization," delves into how to apply a systems mindset to the learning organization and ensure that it remains a strategic partner to the business. Her unique perspective from various industries as well as in her latest consulting role as leader of Designing Your Life for Women provides award-winning concepts that every CLO should embrace.

To align the learning organization to the business around a systems mindset requires the role of the learning leader to evolve. It means focusing equally on building organizational capabilities and on tailoring your design and deployment approach to the company culture. You can provide great value and build strategic learning organizations by stating why learning is important for your employees and your organization, creating a "learning purpose." This then provides a guiding star to define two important aspects of learning that need to be aligned to the unique nature of your company: your learning culture and your learning brand. Defining the purpose of the learning organization also engages employees and aligns and educates them on the professional and organizational benefits of being a continuous learner and the outcomes they can expect as a result.

Andrew Kilshaw, VP of organizational development and learning at Shell and former CLO at Nike, shares expertise on "Supercharging Your Learning Agenda Through Purpose, Culture, and Brand." His perspective on the importance of brand and culture from his award-winning work at Nike is essential for linking learning to a larger business purpose.

Once you've defined your learning purpose, culture, and brand in your organization, what strategies will you follow to enable your employees to interact and engage with learning opportunities and experiences? To upskill and reskill efficiently and effectively, high-performing organizations create a learning ecosystem that's supported by the people, content, technology, data, and governance in the organization as well as its learning culture. Learning leaders can follow actionable steps to ensure this ecosystem facilitates business performance results; foster confidence, creativity, and commitment in your team; align metrics, strategy, and resources to the CEO's agenda; and cultivate continuous improvement.

Marina Theodotou, center director for operations and analytics in workflow learning directorate at the Defense Acquisition University, shares her insights into how people, content, technology, data, and governance represent "The Five Building Blocks of a Learning Ecosystem." DAU has been an award-winning learning organization for many years. Their focus on measurement, the learning context, and successful learning outcomes provides a look inside the U.S. military and its impressive focus on exceptional development of our service members.

People

Successful learning leaders understand that forward-focused learning is not just about setting strategy and vision—it is also about people: winning over stakeholders, building teams, and enlisting leaders to ensure buy-in.

Often even the best learning strategy can go by the wayside if learning leaders do not develop deep, personal connections with the C-suite and other business leaders. Building strong relationships with organizational stakeholders means investing time and energy to connect with them and learning their interests, motives, and concerns before you ask for their commitment. This requires developing a business-first mindset and skill set, eliminating "learning speak" from your conversations with management, and broadening your understanding of and accountability to important business metrics. To strengthen executive commitment, you need to partner with other business leaders, expand your role of domain expertise, and collaborate with management and employees alike to co-own your initiatives. These partnerships demonstrate your commitment to the business and overall company performance: You are a business enabler and are there to ensure they—and the organization—win.

Kevin Wilde, former CLO at General Mills and program manager at GE, shares expertise about how to engage management with your learning agenda. His chapter on "Winning at Shark Tank: How L&D Leaders Really Gain Managment Support" expands on his numerous years as an award-winning CLO and a management confidant. His early years working for Jack Welch at GE provided him with unique experiences with leadership and learning at the famed GE Leadership Development Center at Crotonville.

Learning leaders cannot serve the organization, its leaders, or its workers alone—you need to build a great learning team capable of making your learning organization strategic. You can start with collecting data about business requirements, assessing your own ability to deliver these requirements, and then evaluating the team. The learning leader role requires both a business-operations understanding and a talent development one. Whichever you have, you can leverage your previous experience to grow your acumen in the other. The three skills most needed by learning teams include understanding the customer, practicing agile learning development, and continuously embracing emerging technologies. As a learning leader, you have many opportunities to either build or buy these skills to round out your staff. In all, the team is the gateway to a truly strategic learning organization.

Gale Halsey, VP of HR at Ford Motor Credit Company, in her chapter "The Talent Behind an Award-Winning Learning Team" addresses the tremendous talent and expertise in exceptional learning teams. She shares the importance of hiring and developing learning leaders who enable award-winning learning organizations. These employees are at the epicenter of our learning cultures and we cannot do our great work without them.

The best learning leaders also realize that the learning team doesn't have to stop at the employees within their department. In fact, they seek out other organizational leaders to get involved in the learning that happens throughout the business. Turning leaders into teachers cultivates a learning culture and appeals to your strongest talent. When leaders are willing to invest their precious time preparing and participating in teaching others, they become role models for the rest of the organization and reinforce that development is a priority in the company. Through active teaching, leaders themselves can promote their own learning, improve their ability to self-reflect, and expose employees to the experiences and perspective of successful leaders.

Jayne Johnson, VP of enterprise learning and development at Alkermes and former VP of talent, learning, and organizational development at Keurig Green Mountain and CLO at Deloitte, is one of the world's experts in leadership development. In her chapter "Leaders as Teachers," she divulges the secrets and strategies she created and used to build award-winning leadership development programs and initiatives. Her insights about using leaders as teachers and turning them into learning ambassadors is invaluable in connecting learning to the business. Her insights and perspective are essential for building leadership capabilities in an organization.

Process

Beyond having the vision, strategy, and people for an effective learning organization, learning leaders need to be mindful of their operations and processes. This starts with getting the most out of existing resources and demonstrating how these resources deliver impact to the organization. Learning leaders should also prioritize collaboration and agility in how everyone in the company learns.

While no learning leader would (or should) turn down the opportunity for more resources, the size of your learning budget does not guarantee success. Rather, it is what you do with your resources that matters. Forward-focused learning organizations use a combination of in-house and outsourced learning solutions, content, and technologies to maximize their value to the organization. You should keep your learning strategy simple by focusing on what will achieve the greatest return for the business: The simpler the strategy, the easier it is to explain, maintain, and refine. Above all, using resources wisely continues to move the organization forward.

Michelle Braden, VP of global talent development at Wex and former CLO and VP of global learning excellence at TELUS International, unveils the importance of learning investments and prioritization in her chapter "Do More With Less: Using Your Budget Wisely." Learning investments are continuously scrutinized, and Michelle shares her key lessons and strategies for ensuring that investments of time, money, and resources are effectively implemented. Fiscal responsibility and aligning resources on the most important priorities have enabled her to lead award-winning initiatives.

As aptitude with data analytics and data-based action are vital capabilities for learning professionals, learning leaders should emphasize building the data muscle of their team members from data collection, to data analysis, to data visualization techniques and reporting. To effectively measure where and how development is taking place, you and your team should know how to analyze the organization, discover patterns, and document development. It is the learning leaders' responsibility to take a strategic approach to analyzing and sharing data to prioritize initiatives and optimize the organization's performance.

Martha Soehren, former CTDO at Comcast and SVP of Comcast University, shares how to turn measurement data into usable insights to prove the talent development function's impact on the organization in her chapter "Impact Matters." All the work done by a learning team and learning organization is only effective if it has impact. Martha shares her extensive experience as a thought leader in ensuring her learning function generates critical impact on the organization in this important chapter.

Impact certainly matters. So does thinking outside the box for solutions. One way learning leaders can enable the purpose and values of the organization is to ensure employees build the confidence and skills they require to make the biggest difference. As the workforce becomes more digital, diverse, dispersed, mobile, and flexible, organizations begin to rely on different types of collaboration to solve complex, business-critical problems. Using a framework built around real problems, a structured approach, strong personal commitment to success, networked connections, and inclusive teams, you can prepare employees for collaboration—wherever they are. As with anything you do as a learning leader, you'll need to embrace organizational change, patience and persistence, and a culture that encourages and believes in continuous learning.

Aimee George Leary, global talent officer, **Ruth Almen**, leadership and executive services director, and **Chris Holmes**, functional learning director, all at Booz Allen Hamilton, offer insights about how their company has focused on innovation and collaboration to build their award-winning learning organization in their chapter "Collaborative Learning Drives Collective Ingenuity." They share Booz Allen's Collaborative Learning Framework and examples of how they've put it into practice, such as hackathons, "capture the flag" events, and learning circles.

Old habits die hard. This is true for frontline employees, middle managers, and C-suite executives—and even learning leaders. But learning organizations, and the broader business, demand more agile techniques to respond to pressing day-to-day issues and long-term challenges. Learning leaders can be on the forefront of leading their organization in transforming to an agile culture. You'll need to grow your Agile team, while protecting what works in your existing organization. agile means less "build once and deliver to many" initiatives and more personalized and blended learning approaches—ones that empower the organization to perform at its best, today and in the future. Because process change is hard, you also need to serve as change champion, while providing a vision to rally people around why being an agile learner is foundational to success. Data and analytics can help you respond faster and more accurately.

Annmarie Neal, SVP of employee experience at Ultimate Software, chief talent officer at Hellman & Friedman, and former CLO at Cisco, and **Laura Gentry**, CHRO at Ultimate Software, in their chapter "Agile Is the New Smart" share their company's journey and how they have adopted Agile techniques to build their business. Innovation, business alignment, and commitment to change enabled them to have a big impact on the organization. Their strategies for implementing new ways of thinking and technologies have enabled the business to thrive.

These insights and perspectives span industries, companies, and years of experience spent building award-winning, forward-focused learning organizations. Our profession and industry would not be as progressive or critical to business without their tireless work. I wish to thank all of my highly respected colleagues who contributed their tremendous knowledge and expertise to this book. You continue to inspire with your breakthrough innovations, enviable learning cultures, and compelling business outcomes.

Here's to learning!

1

Becoming a Strategic Business Driver

Brad Samargya

> Business integration is a key priority for all learning organizations. Linking learning strategy to business strategy ensures business impact and longevity of a learning function.

Why is it that when times get tough, learning is one of the first areas to get cut?

Anyone who has spent any length of time in employee learning and development can share tales of valued colleagues no longer here, program budgets cut to a fraction of what they used to be, and travel budgets that have shrunk to the point employees may not even get to meet their managers once a year.

Sound familiar?

This has been my personal observation as a learning leader, and at times my personal experience. Along with many of you, I have ridden the roller coaster of expansion and contraction that inevitably happens to our learning organizations in concert with the business. And many of you have shared your war stories with me.

When the budget axe falls, those of us who survive all wonder what the heck just happened.

Our first reaction is often that the fault lies elsewhere. We are underappreciated victims of a finance-driven spreadsheet exercise. Others are making critical decisions, we are not invited to the party, and we cross our fingers hoping someone will stick up for L&D.

Why are the other departments, especially sales, products, and services, getting all the money while we reduce our investment in our most important asset, our people? It can get a bit tiring, but we can commiserate and take solace from our friends in marketing, HR, and other support organizations who also bear the brunt of the latest round of budget cuts.

Learning leaders need to step up and take responsibility for making learning and development a strategic priority that is protected and valued. During my 20 years of experience as a chief learning officer I have learned this lesson the hard way, and I've developed some best practices I think can help. I break them down to four key actions you can take to achieve a seat at the table as a strategic business driver, essential to the success of your organization.

Step One: Build Staff Capability in Aligning to the Business

I have seen first-hand how senior leaders are overwhelmed with the day-to-day challenges of making their sales quotas, developing their products, and delivering their services, while running from meeting to meeting and customer to customer. I find I want to shout slow down, take a short time out, and let's talk about your employees. It is indeed sometimes difficult to elbow your way into their calendars to talk about employee development and build the relationships you need to be a strategic business advisor—but we must!

And what should you do once you get in front of a business leader? You need to engage with them on their terms. You need to gain credibility starting with establishing that you understand their business priorities and can help support them in achieving their business goals. This starts by engaging in conversations about the business drivers and identifying key dependencies on people and their capabilities to execute the business strategy. To resonate with leaders, you need to talk about strategic competence gaps and needs, not training. This is followed by discussions regarding whether the organization has the talent it needs to be successful, and if not, whether it needs to build or buy those skills.

As a learning organization, aligning your learning team to the business is how you must gain the table stakes to be relevant. It is imperative you align very capable learning partners to each major function, its senior leader, and their leadership team—not an easy feat. This is a tough role to fill, requiring a very talented learning professional with business acumen. Your leader cannot be an order-taker, and they must have credibility! Ideally they are someone with domain experience; they absolutely must be a performance consultant regarding the dimensions of competence and people. They hear their stakeholder's pain but question the true root cause, do not jump immediately to the training solution suggested by the leader, and return with an analysis of the underlying cause or performance issue and a proposed solution that will have real business impact. By the way, if and when cost cuts are coming, not having these relationships and alignment virtually assures a bad outcome for you and your team. That said, organizational alignment should follow the steps presented here to yield any results.

A note here on performance consulting: This is an invaluable skill that I believe every learning professional should have, whether they are business-leader facing or internally facing. If you are not familiar, learn more about the capabilities required as well as some of the great training available to build these skills. The way I find to equate this to learning is a doctor–patient analogy. Simply put, we are not order takers.

If a patient approaches a doctor and tells them they need a major operation, the physician does not order surgery for the next day. She explores with that patient why they think they need the operation, she inquires about the symptoms, she runs tests to gather additional information, she reframes the problem and offers the correct solution, and then she schedules a follow-up to see if the treatment resulted in a positive outcome.

This is no different from the business leader who tells the learning partner, "We are missing our sales number, so we need to train 5,000 people on storytelling skills. Can you start the training next month?" A learning performance consultant will:

» Understand the pain.
» Gain agreement on a next step to engage with stakeholders to better understand the challenge.
» Gain insight into the actual root cause of the business problem (which often is not the one initially identified by the executive).
» Reframe the challenge with the business leader.
» Agree on the proper learning solution as well as how to measure success once executed.

Step Two: Create a Strategic Learning Business Plan

I have been shocked at how many companies have a robust and very resource-intensive annual strategic planning and budget process that lacks a critical component: competence planning. Regarding L&D's role, I call this process "strategy to competence," and I believe it is an essential part of your overall strategic business planning process for each major unit you support. This is best done in partnership with workforce planning and your HR business partner, although I have found it is best for L&D to take the lead in this focused discussion.

Once L&D is organizationally aligned, you must get involved in the strategic planning process, ideally in the form of a formal process working with stakeholders to address some key questions that ultimately result in a strategic learning business plan for that unit. You will know when you have succeeded because it will be owned by the business and formulated with your L&D performance consultant team working with management and backed by resources and budget. The questions are simple; the plans, the formation, and execution are not. Ask:

» What are the major strategic competence gaps that could that prevent us from executing our strategy?

» More specifically, where do these strategic competence gaps exist in terms of job roles, units, and geographies, and what is our plan to ensure we have competent resources in place to sell, develop, or deliver programs to execute against our strategic and operating plans?

» Will we need to build or buy (hire or acquire) this competence to address these gaps?

Don't be surprised if the leadership team you are supporting has not fully thought this through; when they haven't, you will see their business plans fail. After the fact the business will realize that the sales team did not have the competence to effectively position and sell your products, the services organization did not have the competence to deliver the services you sold, or the product organization missed deadlines or produced products with quality issues that affect your customers.

When you pose these questions during the planning process, you may find that your senior leaders do not actually know all the answers, but their people do. This is where L&D's performance consulting skills are really needed. Make sure your team conducts a workplace analysis with mid-level management and especially employee focus groups to identify or validate perceived competence gaps and possible solutions and take these findings back to senior leadership. They will very much appreciate that the plans are grounded in research and discovery within their teams.

Personally, I take great pleasure in working with the business in partnership to craft these plans and my L&D team does as well. It is rewarding and very interesting.

So, a lot of hard work is done to craft a solid strategic learning plan. But a plan is not enough; you must get senior leadership of that unit and their leadership team to understand and sign off on that plan. The way I have done this is gain agreement with the business leader to speak at their next leadership team meeting. With their sponsorship, you can present the strategic learning plan supporting the business strategy with clearly identified strategic competence gaps, and then share the learning plans to address those gaps.

With leadership, it's important that you make it clear that the strategic learning plans resulting from this process are the business's plans, not L&D's. Yes, you will step up and execute, but you need the input of subject matter experts to develop the solutions and the support of management to drive adoption along with the funding needed to make it happen. This ensures an interlock with leadership and ownership by them and creates a clear interdependency on learning for the success of their strategy and achievement of their operating plans.

When this is done well, you may find your budget and resources for next year substantially increase because you are interlocked with the business and have strong executive supporters who include competence development as a key part of their strategy and plans for the coming year.

Step Three: Use the Plans to Back Up Your Budget

Is this strategic planning process I recommend a guarantee your budget will be approved? No. But in good times as well as tough times the business leadership will be the first to support L&D's plans with finance when you are aligned to their strategy and have done this well. I have had the CFO on several occasions push me to cut my budget substantially and had the business leaders and even the CEO back me up and support our plans.

Let me share more here about an approach that has worked quite well for me in the past when given a very difficult budget target to achieve during challenging times. We all need to make tough calls when asked to reduce budgets, and L&D will likely have to do its part. I recall in a prior role in a very difficult year, all leaders had to significantly reduce spending. The preliminary target I was given was far too drastic a reduction and I knew it would hurt the business and its future. The CFO and finance team were not in the mood to debate, and I had a number to meet.

Rather than cut to the CFO's number, I put together a summary spreadsheet with total L&D expense from the prior year followed by rows of cuts that I would need to make to achieve the new target from finance. These reductions I divided into three sections using the colors of a stoplight:

» green, which were program cuts that were tough but I proposed we should make given our financial challenges
» yellow, which were flagged as a "caution," which would materially affect the business and management needed to have a full awareness of that impact before making the cuts
» red, which I called "cutting to the bone marrow," that I recommended we do not do as they would severely hurt the company but would be cut if we were held to the target.

I called the CEO and asked to meet face to face. I told him I could achieve my new target but was very concerned and wanted to discuss the impact of each reduction and get his buy-in to the plan. I told him I could not make these decisions on my own knowing the potential effects to the business. In the end, we agreed on the green cuts, which I made. Surprisingly, he said we should not make many of the yellow cuts, but most importantly he agreed we could not make any of the red cuts as they would cripple our business. He actually cut less than I had planned. Later it only took a two-minute conversation with the CFO to agree on my final target, because he understood the decisions were based on business impact. I could not have had this discussion without first having solid plans in place. The key was involving leadership in the tough decisions and making them aware of the potential impact to their business.

Now on to recommendation number four.

Step Four: Maintain Continuous Engagement With the Business

To maintain the partnership with the business and engagement with senior management, it is critical you deliver the learning plans you have jointly developed and, just as importantly, stay actively engaged with senior leadership on an ongoing basis. You need them to understand the status of the strategic learning initiatives, assist in mitigating any barriers or risks, and engage them in change communications and driving adoption. In return, they expect to hear back from L&D about the results and business impact. This regular interaction year to year will ensure that leadership continues to value the L&D function as a key business partner and competence development as a critical component of their operating plans.

To continue this productive relationship, I recommend quarterly, or at the very least semi-annual, meetings with the senior executive leader and more regular updates with their leadership team or your key business sponsor. There are obviously many reasons for this, including continued visibility and support. Most importantly, the L&D team can reinforce the message that these plans are strategic, they are owned by the business unit, and the leadership needs to ensure continued involvement. This is your ticket to regular interaction to keep employee development on the agenda. When done well, visibility for L&D significantly increases with your senior leaders.

One technique my team has successfully employed was to complement the periodic status review and planning sessions leading into each fiscal year with a semi-annual feedback loop. Why? In the past I found out too late when stakeholders were not happy or did not value what we did; it usually came as a surprise, and often during tough budget discussions when leaders did not support the L&D team assigned to them. Of course, if someone is not happy, you want to find out immediately and course correct.

We designed a process where we asked our business stakeholders to provide feedback on our performance and inserted this into the goals of the L&D strategic business lead as well as our entire L&D leadership team. We asked the overall leader and those members of their leadership team we were closely supporting to measure us on a scale of one to five on the following criteria, which we tracked over time:

» Do we understand your business?
» Do we provide proactive business advice with regard to competence development?
» Do we craft strategic learning plans that meet your needs?
» Do we develop quality learning solutions?
» Do we measure and report back results?

We found that this feedback mechanism was invaluable. No surprise, not everyone is pleased with L&D. In fact, I have employed this technique several times, and each time our scores were initially disappointing but showed continuous improvement to the point we soon averaged excellent scores.

By asking this range of questions it means that we are measuring more than just learning completions. It means we are identifying whether L&D is in tune with the business and able to make an impact. It provides the opportunity for L&D to show progression as well and increasing alignment with the business.

Within my team, we agreed to use the process as a positive measure and not punitive, because when it was first introduced my team was nervous. No one was penalized for a poor score (and yes, we had some). Interestingly, we also had some strong supporters who suddenly dropped their scores over time. What we did value and execute very well was that we would listen to the why of the poor rating and agree on an action plan with that leader. In most instances this led to them becoming our best supporters. I recall one leader saying in their entire career they had never had a support function ask the business to rate them and wished all other support organizations would be brave enough to do the same. And last but not least, this gave us another tangible measure of our stakeholder satisfaction scores and value to the business to report to our own leadership.

Litmus Test on L&D Alignment

In summary, a quick way to measure how well aligned you are to the business would be how well your senior business leaders can answer yes or no to the following:

» I know and value my L&D strategic business partner.
» I have a strategic learning plan that supports by strategy and operating plans.
» I have partnered with the learning team to secure the budget and resources within L&D or in my unit needed to execute my learning plans.
» I am actively engaged with my leadership team to drive the change communications and adoption needed for these plans to yield positive outcomes.
» I see results and will continue to engage L&D to support my business.

2

Designing an Effective Learning Organization

Susan Burnett

> One size fits one. The right model is highly dependent on your business strategy and leadership commitment.

After building more than 10 enterprise-wide learning organizations in five different companies, all in different industries, my successes and failures have resulted in many key lessons learned and a methodology for success. Some of these lessons are informed by research and organizational models, others from the school of hard knocks, proving the research on high flyers (McCall 1998). Challenging assignments and lessons learned from experience have always been the most powerful source of my own learning and growth.

In every company, while the approach was the same, the actual learning and talent management (L&TM) organization's strategy, structure, roles, processes, systems, and metrics were different. They were all designed in tight alignment with the business strategy and organization design, which by nature meant each company required a different solution. Every company has a different business model and is in a different phase of maturity. Every leadership team is driving unique initiatives for transformation and growth. Every L&TM organization must be designed to deliver the solutions that the organization needs to achieve its goals. My first key lesson was that one size, in fact, fits one.

In this chapter, I'll show how you can apply a systems mindset to the learning organization and ensure that it remains a strategic partner to the business.

Lesson 1: Start Transformation at Home

When I entered Hewlett-Packard, Gap, Deloitte, and Yahoo! as a new leader to drive talent management and organization development strategies, I was consistently confronted with a huge gap between the current work of the L&TM teams and the needs of the business. In my one-on-ones with my new team, I would inevitably hear how they were committed to being strong business partners, yet they were perceived as disconnected from the business at best and irrelevant at worst. As I dug in and collaborated with my team, the HR team, and business leaders to assess the current state of my own organization, I quickly learned the disconnect was systemic and not about the individual players.

This drives my conviction that transformation work starts at home, with your own organization, your people, and yourself. You must start with an objective assessment of your team's strategy, its structure, the processes and systems you use to get work done, your people's capabilities and interests, and the culture of your organization. And you have to know yourself—the strengths you bring and the areas you need to shore up with other's expertise. Your mindset should be open and curious, so you can learn what's unique about the company you have joined.

In my first 30 days in any new role, I meet with the key leaders and most influential people in the organization. I want to learn why customers need our products and services and what really differentiates us in the marketplace. I want to better understand the business model and how we make money. I need to know each leader's priorities and what they see as the obstacles to success. I read business plans. I review the company's P&L to identify our biggest costs. All this knowledge is critical if you are really going to be a business partner.

I also want to know the track record of HR and my team, so I know what to change to improve our performance. People tend to tell a new leader the good, the bad, and the ugly, because you bring no loyalties, defensiveness, or baggage to the conversation. When I wasn't new to an organization, if I couldn't be perceived as neutral and objective, I hired a consultant to help me do the assessment. Most of all, I wanted to resist doing what made me successful in the past. This is a pothole I've fallen into before, and I've seen it cripple many new leaders. It's worth emphasizing: *Resist defaulting to your past formula for success.* It may not be what is required for today or the future.

The tricky work of being a great business partner is transforming your own organization while at the same time working with the business leaders to accelerate the larger transformation for the company. I often hear learning leaders talk about this challenge as changing the wheels on the car while driving at high speed. This has never made sense to me. You can't actually change wheels on a moving car! My metaphor is practical. Physician, heal yourself first. You can't meet with patients and do your best healing work when you are sick. Make sure your own organization and leaders are healthy and ready for the long hours of business, culture, and people transformation work that lies ahead.

Lesson 2: Focus on the System

Systems produce what they are designed to produce. If the L&TM organization is a system tuned to deliver whatever someone requests, then that's what it produces—a highly responsive request-fulfillment organization. To understand the system I was walking into, I always built a current state assessment using Jay Galbrath's Star Model (Figure 2-1). Why? Because it examines how all elements of an organization work together in a system that produces desired results. If parts of the system are broken or not aligned to the strategy, the organization isn't healthy and there is usually friction in how it operates.

FIGURE 2-1. Jay Galbrath's Star Model: Organizations Are Systems

Direction
- Vision and Mission
- Customer and Product Priorities
- Markets to Be Served
- Competitive Advantage
- Business Goals and Strategies

Strategy

Skills and Mindsets
- Jobs and Roles
- Recruiting
- Selection
- Learning and Development
- Build vs. Buy

People

Culture
The way we do things here: values, beliefs, behaviors, attitudes

Decision-Making Power
- Hierarchy, Spans, and Layers
- Centralization vs. Decentralization
- Alignment
- Decision Making
- Networks
- Physical Environment

Structure

Incentives
- Success Scorecard
- Salaries
- Bonus Structures
- Promotions
- Accountability
- Recognition

Rewards

Processes

Information
- Clear, Documented, Automated, and Owned Business Processes
- Horizontal Processes and Linking Mechanisms
- Networks

The Star Model requires you to deeply understand the business strategy, and then examine the alignment or misalignment of the structures, processes, rewards, people, and culture that exist to execute that strategy. When new executives change the strategy, they must change the key organization elements that were tuned to enable a different strategy. Too often, executives focus only on structure, changing the boxes on an org chart and the names within those boxes. But this is only one part of a six-part system that has to be designed to accelerate the strategy and aligned to be a self-reinforcing and efficient system. What about the processes and systems that exist to support a different strategy? What about the measures? And most importantly, is the culture going to enable or disable the new strategy?

Build the Learning Organization System

Let's make this real with an example. In 2000, Hewlett-Packard was a highly decentralized company with four large business units, each the size of a medium-size company. They all had their own CEOs and executive teams, functions, and geographies. We were in 170 countries and had region leaders who were the single interface to the customer, often bringing together the assets of multiple business units for large global deals. Like any other large company, we had a matrixed organization. Based on this system design, it was no surprise that the L&TM function was also highly decentralized. We had more than 75 organizations of varying sizes, focus, and capabilities located in geographies, functions, business units, and corporate.

A new CEO and executive team arrived and began to examine everything in the company for efficiency, effectiveness, and return on investment. The spotlight was on enabling functions, also known as unpopular overhead on the expense line. The CFO began to assess the L&TM functions across the company, trying to figure out the total cost envelope. His question was simple: "How much are we spending on all this stuff and what's the ROI?"

Since I had worked with him in the past as the head of executive development, he asked me to help him think through how to find all these costs. After our first meeting and a discussion with the CEO and CHRO, we framed four key questions:

 » How much was Hewlett-Packard investing in learning and talent management as a company?
 » How much of that investment was building the most competitive workforce and leaders in the world?
 » How much was directly tied to our company, business, function, and geographic business goals and strategies?
 » Were we getting the best return on our investment?

At the time, I was in marketing in the Computer Systems Organization. One of my responsibilities was sales force training and performance support, which meant I led one of the 75 L&TM organizations in the company. Since there was no single learning or talent management line item in my budget, or the budgets across the company, we had to comb through the general ledger and identify costs buried in other expense line items. Determining your total spend on L&TM people and programs is a critical step in becoming a business asset.

Our approach at HP typified the company's culture at the time. The CFO emailed all the heads of L&TM organizations he could find and invited them to join a task force to help answer these questions. The goal was to objectively assess the current state of L&TM across the company and make recommendations for how the function could improve its ROI. Forty leaders around the globe volunteered to be part of this team. I credit HP's culture of openness, transparency, and collaboration for a thorough current state assessment and a future state recommendation, with minimal self-serving behaviors and unhealthy politics. Figure 2-2 is a STAR Model summary of this work.

FIGURE 2-2. HP Current State Assessment and Future State Recommendation, Fiscal Year 2000

As you can see on the left side for each point in the star, the current state was set up to support a mission that was all about being responsive to business manager's requests for the programs they thought their teams needed. They self-funded all their efforts by charging back those managers, or in some cases the individuals who participated. The organizations felt entrepreneurial and were proud of their ability to fund their headcount and programs. The structure, processes, and systems supported manager surveys, contracts with managers, deliveries of training (often by a manager or HR leader's favorite vendor), and a sophisticated charge-back system. (The CFO discovered the cost of charging back to individual location codes was in the millions!) The key metrics were all about individual employee and manager satisfaction and repeat business.

After many interviews with executives and guidance from the CEO and CFO, we knew we had to shift this function to a new mission (see the right side for each point in the star of Figure 2-2). The task force agreed we needed an organization that would "Develop the most competitive workforce and leaders in the world, building the capabilities needed to compete and win in every market we serve." Once we made this decision, the L&TM system had to be re-designed to make it happen. Instead of manager surveys on training needs, we needed to have business governance bodies that defined the critical capabilities necessary to achieve the business strategy and fiscal year goals. The structure needed to parallel the business structure and report in at higher levels. We consolidated fragmented, small L&TM organizations at the business unit, function, geography, and corporate levels. We also needed to define what should be centralized at the enterprise level. New jobs were created at higher levels for the strategic partnership and consulting that was needed to define a workforce and organization plan that would enable the business strategy and fiscal year priorities. The entire system changed to enable the new mission.

Lesson 3: Ensure the L&TM Mission Enables the Business Mission

The HP example illustrates how critical it is for the L&TM function to have a clear mission that defines what it will and will not do. And the mission must resonate with business leaders and communicate that your function is there to enable their mission.

At Yahoo!, our new company mission was to be a digital media leader enabled by great technology. After meeting with the executive team and working with them on their strategy, it became clear that my L&TM organization had to get out of the training business of offering lots of courseware, and into the capability-building business. We were small, we had a limited budget, and our mantra was "If it doesn't enable the strategy or transformation, we don't do it!" As a result, I was able to cancel a $500,000 contract with an e-learning vendor providing a library of courseware and redirect that money to talent strategies that would build the new management, leadership, and culture changes required for our success. Mission drove priorities and investments.

Deloitte is another great example of the power of a well-crafted mission. I was hired at Deloitte to build Deloitte University (DU)—the total system. This was a start-up. I got to define the strategy, design a new structure, build core processes and systems, and work with architects, partners, and contractors to build the corporate university. I hired the CLOs who would make it happen and created the governance and scorecard to measure success and keep us on track.

After the current state assessment and many interviews with partners across the firm, it became clear that our mission was to "Ensure Deloitte professionals were client-ready faster and more effectively than our competitors." With this mission, we prioritized the onboarding of new hires as our first firm-wide talent initiative and a showcase of our DU strategy for leading-edge learning. That got us to work with partners in each business unit to identify the skills, behaviors, and mindset of a "client-ready new hire." We also engaged them in the assessment of our new hires against these new criteria. We began to measure how many new hires were endorsed as "client-ready" and how long it took to get them there. It didn't surprise me that we reduced the time it took. Measuring your ability to deliver on your mission will always galvanize your team to deliver these results.

Too often, I work with HR, learning, and talent management leaders in companies and their missions are basically the same. All say in some form, "We will deliver great HR services and solutions that enable the business." You could put any logo on this mission. Who doesn't want to provide great services and solutions? But this mission doesn't provide the strategic direction and boundaries needed to decide priorities. It doesn't communicate the unique value that will be delivered to the business. A mission drives focus. It also drives investments. Even better, it drives how you measure success.

Lesson 4: Design Your Structure and Key Processes for Business Alignment

With the strategy in place, the next step is to define the structure that will best execute that strategy, without regard to the current roles and people in them. This is where you have to take on the perspective of an external consultant or actually hire one to help you. You must be objective and data-driven to build a structure and set of roles that support the work to be done and align with the way the business is organized.

At Gap I joined an L&D team that delivered "programs driven by the business." This meant a business leader had asked them to do a program and they delivered it, using the vendors the business leader preferred. As a result, we had duplication of effort, multiple contracts with the same vendor, and conflicting programs. For example, the company had four different leadership development programs, all focused on different capabilities, using unique vocabularies, with varying levels of success and management support. It's hard to build the leadership capabilities needed to compete and win with a new company strategy if you are operating this way.

When we decided the mission of our organization was "to enable the successful execution of the new Gap strategy and culture for growth," I had to create a new structure and define new roles. I renamed our organization Talent Management and Strategic Change and created a new department in my team of strategic change consultants. It's also worth noting that in every company I joined, I had to accomplish these structural changes with the same or reduced level of headcount. I quickly learned how to repurpose existing headcount and spend, based on what the business valued and needed most. Start from scratch and build the organization that's needed.

At Gap, we needed a strategic change role to support the CEO to drive the company and business changes necessary for the growth strategy's success. I created a new senior director of strategic change role for my leadership team and opened up the job internally and externally. Since we had never hired for this skill set, I had no internal applicants and ended up hiring a great external leader. She and I quickly built a team of change and organization development (OD) consultants who worked dotted line for the business and solid line for this center of expertise. It was critical that the brand leaders saw this strategic change consultant as their go-to resource for the talent, organization, and culture initiatives that would help them achieve their aggressive growth goals. It was also critical that the CEO saw that he had a set of resources that would assist the brand presidents to execute the company-wide changes the executive leadership team had agreed upon. Dual reporting was a great structure to accomplish both goals—tight alignment with the business as well as tight alignment between me and the business line working on the company agenda. No silos allowed.

I did the same with my L&D team. Formerly they were organized by programs: executive, management, and a few employee programs. I organized them by business unit as their primary focus, so they could be the voice of the business and the connection to the company's strategy and leaders. Their job was to work directly with the HR and brand leadership teams to define the needed business and company capabilities. Once they had an agreed upon the learning and organization development annual plan, they built unique programs for the business and executed them with speed, quality, and alignment.

Dual Reporting Works!

I use dual reporting frequently to achieve alignment, so it's worth commenting on how to use it well. In every company I was in, I wanted to make sure there was a close connection in real time and all the time between my team and the business team at the right level.

- At HP, I structured the L&TM organization the way the company was structured. The heads of L&TM worked for the heads of HR in the business, functions, and geographies (dotted line) and for me (solid line).
- At Deloitte, I created CLOs for every business unit, because the firm used independent business units as its organizing principle. The CLOs worked for me (solid line) and a partner designated to lead talent (dotted line).
- At Yahoo! my leaders worked for the HR leaders in the functions and geographies, because that's how Yahoo! was structured. While I had the solid line reporting, I made sure the dotted line leader and I jointly managed the CLOs. We did their annual goals and plans, annual budgets, quarterly check-ins, and annual performance reviews together.

It's hard to work at cross-purposes or have your leader be pulled in two different directions when you have this clear management alignment.

Decision Making

To stay aligned and make good business decisions, I used some core decision-making processes. First, I always worked with the HR business partners to set up a governance body for the business units, functions, and geographies to help shape and manage accountability for the annual L&TM plan. In many cases, this was the most significant spend in the HR budget; therefore I always argued that the decisions regarding priorities and investments must be made by business leaders, not just HR. At Deloitte, it was a body of the most influential and experienced partners, because they could influence the organization to support Deloitte University plans and priorities. At Gap, it was high-potential executives, because the CEO and executive leadership team positioned this governance as an important enterprise development experience for high-potential leaders.

The one golden rule I used with all governance bodies was the need for business sponsorship for any initiative to become a priority. If someone was proposing an initiative as part of the annual plan and investment, I required a business leader (or team of leaders, even better) to sponsor the initiative. Sponsorship means that that person advocates for the initiative with you when presenting to executive teams, removes obstacles, secures support, and leads the charge. Many proposed initiatives didn't get funded because they didn't have sponsors who met these requirements.

At Deloitte, we built a new and different L&D strategy that required experiential, leading-edge learning enabled by next-generation technology. Our rule was we only funded those initiatives and programs that supported or showcased this strategy. This meant some of the proposals by partners who were living in the old paradigm of conferences and festivals of PowerPoint presentations didn't get funded. The CLOs and governance bodies had rallied around the new Deloitte University strategy and were putting their money where their mouth was. Remember, she who has the gold makes the rules.

Financial Planning and Reporting

The other core process I always designed was the financial planning and reporting process. At HP, Deloitte, Gap, and Yahoo! the budget was centralized, and I owned how the L&TM money would get allocated to the businesses, functions, geographies, and corporate organizations. In all cases, if I didn't have a transparent, business-driven way of allocating money to priorities, I was setting myself up for failure.

Here are the fundamental questions I worked with my leadership teams to answer:

» What's the right level of total investment in learning and talent management? In other words, how big is the pie?

» How will we decide how much money each unit gets out of the total budget? How much pie does everyone get?

» How will we decide which company-wide initiatives to fund? What kind of pies are we making?

» How will we decide how much to invest in shared services such as infrastructure, systems, and tools? What kind of pie crust do we need, and how much should we make?

» How will we manage the month-to-month actual spending on a use-it-or-lose-it basis? How do we make sure we don't waste our pie?

Let's tackle each of these questions on their own.

How big is the overall talent and organization development budget—your pie?

Having been on the board of ATD (formerly ASTD) and a member of the benchmarking forum, I always used the ATD benchmark as a starting point for any conversation about the total investment in learning and development. Defining the overall budget as either a percent of payroll investment or development dollars per employee is a great way to start the financial conversation of "How much is enough?" Once you have that number, line up the strategy, and develop your three-year plan, you have the reality of what you can get done every year. I always created a three-year plan so the executive teams could see how the investments flowed year to year, and I didn't have to make a new business case for a budget each year.

At Deloitte, we actually created a professional services benchmark working with ATD, our DU governance body, and all my CLOs. We decided to invest "among the leaders," which put us at about a 3 percent of payroll investment. This became our budget each year. At Yahoo! I worked with the CEO and CFO to determine the key initiatives we needed to get done over a three-year period, priced that, and then checked it against a percent of payroll investment tuned to high-tech companies in growth or transformation mode. When I was determining the investment in sales force development at HP, I worked with my executive team to define how much we wanted to invest in sales reps and managers and compared it against the investment per person benchmark for technology companies. No matter what rubric I used, it was one co-created with the CFO and endorsed by the governance body or executive team.

A budget, like any other part of the system, is just an indicator of what is valued. When I inherit a budget that is all headcount and very little program dollars, I know that full-time headcount was highly valued in the past. When the budget is mostly program dollars, I know that buying the current and best capabilities in the market is highly valued. Since a budget is only an artifact of the past, I always start my budgeting process with a clean sheet of paper and build it from scratch. By starting from a zero base, you are making sure the budget will deliver the resources you need to execute your strategy, operate within the three-year and annual plans, and stay within the total cost envelope you have defined.

How will we decide how much money each unit gets out of the total budget? How much pie does everyone get?

The temptation for most leaders is to take the total budget and divide it equally among all the units. Other leaders will allocate the dollars to each unit based on their head-count, rationalizing that larger organizations need more money. In my experience, both are ineffective ways of distributing the budget.

At HP we answered this question by matching the business model and strategy to the different units and determining the right percent of payroll investment for each unit. We worked with ATD's benchmarking forum to organize a benchmark for each kind of business, knowing that a highly people-intensive professional services business was very different than a consumer-focused, Lean and Agile PC business. The percent of payroll was agreed upon by the governance bodies and translated into their portion of the company-wide budget.

At Deloitte, I pushed the majority of the centralized budget to the business units because that was where most of the transformation to the Deloitte University strategy was going to occur. That meant every CLO for the business created a DU plan and budget co-created and approved by their BU governance bodies and executive teams. A governance body comprising partners from every major unit in the firm identified the firm-wide initiatives the businesses needed to implement, often with CEO spon-sorship. Since the total learning investment didn't get larger during the financial crisis years, the only way to get a bigger piece of the pie was to convince the DU governance bodies that your priorities were central to the success of your BU and the firm. It was quite a dance!

How will we decide which company-wide initiatives to fund? What kind of pies are we making?

My first principle regarding corporate organizations is that they exist solely to support the company-wide strategy, the company's change agenda, and the capabilities the company needs to be successful. Those investments have to be endorsed by the CEO and their executive team, because no one believes "corporate is here to help," and most business leaders want the majority of the money devoted to their priorities.

In the HP example, all the money was distributed to the businesses on paper, and then they had to decide, with their governance bodies, which company-wide initiatives they needed to fund, support, and execute. It's easy when it's a CEO mandate; it goes in the budget. It's harder when it has to supersede business priorities. The corporate budget has to be agreed upon by all the business units, functions, and geographies because it requires their engagement and sponsorship. I also learned that it was critical to drive only a few (think no more than three) big initiatives that the whole company is behind.

How will we decide how much to invest in shared services? What kind of pie crust and how much should we make?

Shared services have become the stepchild in the HR or L&TM organization. We've forgotten that these are cost-effective ways to deliver high-quality and necessary services and expertise that can be leveraged across a whole organization and scaled up or down as demand fluctuates. Having every one of HP's 75 L&TM organizations run their own LMS is inefficient and expensive and delivers unreliable quality. Remember that story of decentralized learning and development units? We had multiple and different LMS implementations across the company, resulting in many gaps and overlaps such as:

> » different versions of the same software platform, with no one organization investing in staying current and rolling to future versions (this was a pre-cloud world)
> » multiple contracts with the same vendor
> » three different vendor platforms in use, all with different contracts and varying capabilities and quality levels
> » no seamless transfer of employee records
> » no easy way to implement cross-company registration and reporting
> » people were doing duplicate work
> » variable quality, with no single instance that was industry current or best-in-class
> » ridiculously high LMS costs and low levels of functionality.

To determine the shared services budget, I like to treat this as if I were an external vendor with formal contracts and transparent prices. I ask my teams to identify the services the businesses need. Once we have the services list, we establish criteria for quality, performance, and cost, all based on benchmarks for these services in the outside world. Then we form contracts with the units for what they want to buy.

We always have some infrastructure services they can't opt out of, like an LMS, performance management system, employee survey, and so on. A pie has to have a crust. Those key infrastructure mandates are usually defined and sponsored by the HR leaders in the organization. Once the contracts are completed, we set up a management reporting and quarterly review process that is critical to keep the units engaged in the value and benefit of their shared services. I always measured my shared services organizations based on their ability to exceed the expectations defined in the contracts, and they did a great job of giving the units insights into how the services were being used by their employees. We ran shared services like a business.

How do you allocate the costs of shared services? There are multiple ways to set up a shared service buying process. At HP, once the units had their contracts, we charged them based on the price for the service and their total headcount. When I ran a marketing organization that served the field, the region sales leaders chose how much they wanted to buy from a menu of sales support services. This gets tricky because usage is an estimate. For example, the sales leaders would always underestimate how many executive briefings they needed annually, so we had to have a way to contract for more or fewer services in real time (price per customer visit) and still balance our budgets.

Whatever rubric you use, I recommend a formal contract with the businesses for the services they need, the metrics that will indicate success or failure, and the quarterly reporting that will drive accountability. It's worth the time and effort. Leaders who make choices about the shared services they want to buy tend to advocate for the shared services organization and don't see them as a transactional spend to reduce every year.

Lesson 5: Get the Right People in the Right Roles at the Right Time

We're in the talent business, so we should understand that talent is the key to our success. If this is true, then why is it that when you join a new company or get promoted you also inherit legacy leaders, average performers, some who didn't play well with others, and some who didn't have the skills or mindset needed to accomplish the new mission? When this happens, I have learned I must act quickly to get the right people in the right roles or I will fail. I've watched leaders wait too long to replace a leader on their team who isn't a match, and it derails progress at best and leads to failure at worst. You are only as strong as your weakest leader.

I spend the first 90 days in a new organization assessing my people against the new roles and requirements that are driven by the mission, strategy, and structure choices we've made. My job is to match my leaders to the roles where they will excel. Since the structure requires new roles, I always post those openings and let all internal and external candidates apply, so we can get the best person for the job. This is especially helpful for incumbents, as they get feedback on their capabilities and mindset not only from me but from business leaders and HR business partners. If they get the role, they are endorsed and supported by the key players. If they don't get the role, I help them find a job in another part of the organization or outside the company. This is hard, but I've learned it only gets harder if people are in jobs where they can't perform to the new requirements.

I have always loved sports as a spectator and a player, and I have learned from great coaches. For example, the brilliance of Steve Kerr, the Golden State Warriors coach, is his ability to assemble a very talented and deep bench. All the players are high performers, all with unique skills and strengths that make them great additions to the team. Kerr configures the team differently based on who he is competing against. He knows that speed counts more in some situations and height counts more in others. The players work together as a team better than most, because they know what role they play and what strengths they can count on from each other, and they constantly give feedback, learn, and adjust on the court. There is no relative ranking or bell curve here. If an individual doesn't perform in a game, they get less game time or even get benched. If the gaps in their performance continue, they are traded for a player who brings the skills and performance the team needs. You can be an empathetic and development-oriented leader as well as be objective and quick to match the right talent to the right job, and offboard people who can't deliver the capabilities and performance you need to be successful.

I learned this lesson the hard way, and I've never forgotten it. When HP merged with Compaq, I was the head of enterprise talent and organization development. Remember how I had built a new mission, new strategy, and new team? In our first year, we were implementing new initiatives sponsored by the CEO and executive team, and we were driving L&TM solutions that were part of the business agenda. We were getting great results and had saved the company over $100 million in redundant and unnecessary costs.

Fast forward to the merger of HP and Compaq, and the CEO's decision to assemble an A team from both companies. As a result, all the executives in HP and Compaq lost their jobs and were asked to interview for new jobs. The next levels down were selected by the new leadership teams during a fast-start process that included a data-driven talent review.

I interviewed for a new and bigger TM executive role along with my Compaq counterpart, and I got the job. A week later I found myself in a conference room with a new HR leadership team that was half HP and half Compaq. Our job was to design the new HR organization for HP and to select the next level of HR leaders for the new roles we had defined. This was a serious, high-stakes talent review. We were selecting the HR leaders for the future, knowing half of our current leaders would either lose their jobs or be asked to take a different role.

As the Compaq leaders introduced me to their top talent, I was struck by the fact that some of their A players had skills and experience my folks didn't have. In fact, some of their A players were even better than mine! The assessments we used to select our teams were objective, candid, fair, and very detailed. At that moment, I realized that my loyalty to my team had colored my assessment of who was even an A player. The criteria for leadership in the new HP made it clear that some of my folks were B or even C players who had long tenure at HP and were well liked. Tenure, likability, and legacy relationships were no longer the criteria we were using.

At the end of three days, I walked away with a new leadership team that was half Compaq, all of whom I had never met in person. Over the three years of our work together, I realized that having an A team changes the game. Everyone is a high performer, they are matched to a role where they excel, and their initiative and results exceeded my highest expectations. That HP team was one of the strongest I have ever had the privilege of leading.

Lesson 6: Connect Your Metrics to How the Business Measures Success

I'm always surprised when HR, learning, and talent management leaders don't measure their results like any other organization in the business. Having spent 11 years in marketing and sales support, where we measured everything, I just don't get why measurement is missing in this space. When I go to conferences, I continue to hear from talent and learning leaders that it's just too hard to measure how they influence the business because of all the intervening variables that surround performance. I think our profession is making this too difficult or just living in a grand excuse. A marketing leader could say, "It's too difficult to measure whether a marketing campaign creates more brand awareness," but they don't. They define the business result, create the initiatives they think will achieve that result, and take the credit when they move the needle. And when they don't move the needle, they do a root cause analysis, figure out where their assumptions were faulty, define what went wrong, and course correct. It's not about covering your rear; it's about learning from a failure and creating a more effective action quickly and effectively.

As a result of this experience in marketing, it's no surprise that I start metrics work by defining the results business leaders are measuring as part of their strategies and annual plan. Then, my team and I target the metrics where we believe a L&TM solution could have the greatest impact. In all cases, we found the solution was never a single training program. If we really wanted to achieve a business result, we had to build a performance support solution that would pull all the levers that would increase performance. Often, business leaders don't think about all these levers, so you have to be a great consultant. You may even have to shape the way the business actually measures results. At Gap, Yahoo! and HP, I gave input on and helped share the company's balanced scorecard, with an eye to how we could tie to these key metrics.

Measure What Matters

In every case, designing the total solution and metrics was a collaborative effort with business sponsors and HR business partners. Without these key players, the changes required in some of those levers like job design, performance evaluation, compensation, management processes, and training and development won't happen. Table 2-1 presents some tangible examples.

TABLE 2-1. Examples of Learning Solutions and Results

Business Result	L&D or OD Solution	Our Results
HP Major Account Sales Goal Increase size of deal and decrease time to deal close **Metric** Major account managers increase their average deal size and decrease their average time to close a deal based on measurements before and after AMP implementation starts.	**AMP** • New account management process (AMP) is sponsored by the SVP of major accounts. • AMP training occurs on the tools and the new process for sales managers first and account managers second. • Requirement to apply AMP to current deals and share their plan with manager is enacted. • Manager accountability through monthly reviews of AMP plans and progress is implemented. • New metric is available on the sales scorecard that measures the size and time of deals. • Compensation shifts from quarterly to annual targets to eliminate short-term behaviors.	• Increased average size of deal by about 46 percent. Note: We even had some account managers who doubled their deal size and credited the AMP process—that's a wow! • Faster time to deal by an average of 25 days.
Gap CEO and Executive Leadership Team's (ELT) Goal Ensure our executive team can execute the new Gap growth strategy with speed and excellence **Metric** Business execution decisions are made in alignment with the new strategy	**Leading Businesses at Gap** • New model of what it takes to be a successful Gap executive launched, which included behaviors, knowledge, and mindset. • The ELT defined 48 critical strategy execution decisions and then generated and scored alternatives to clearly define what success looked like. • A simulation of the new Gap was created with an external vendor, and all executives ran that simulated company for three years, making those 48 decisions each year. • We scored business execution decision making year over year.	• 100 percent of the executives who completed the simulation increased their strategy execution and decision-making performance. • 100 percent agreed, "I feel confident I can execute the new Gap strategy." • ELT assessment of final business presentations resulted in the validation that all had increased their understanding, communication, and execution of the new Gap strategy.

At the end of the day, if you don't measure your impact on the business, you can't be a business partner. Measure what matters to your business leaders and report on your results. Even better, get embedded in the way the business measures results, and become part of the business scorecard.

Lesson 7: Culture Eats Everything

Peter Drucker is often quoted saying "culture eats strategy for breakfast." Culture is the lynchpin of the organization system; it doesn't just eat breakfast, it eats everything! It's no accident that Jay Galbraith put culture in the center of the Star model. When strategy changes, the culture has to be aligned to support the new mission and set of priorities or you will fail. Full stop. Failure.

I define culture as "the way we do things here." It's easy to see a culture when you look through the eyes of a new hire. You've been there. You know you watch what people say and do to figure out what's tolerated and what's not acceptable. Imagine my surprise when I joined a new company and saw the F-word on slides and heard it in management presentations. What I discovered was we had a CEO who could swear like a sailor. This behavior was totally accepted and deemed cool. Leaders set the tone and shape the culture in their actions and words every moment of the day.

So, how do you change culture? Here's where I use a model that works for me no matter where I go. It's called the "Results Pyramid" (Figure 2-3) developed by Partners in Leadership, and working with them, we taught this model to all our Yahoo! leaders so they could lead and reinforce cultural changes. The premise of this model is that culture lives in the experiences and beliefs that prevail in the organization.

FIGURE 2-3. The Results Pyramid

To understand the Results Pyramid, start at the bottom. Experiences shape your beliefs. Beliefs drive the actions you take. Those actions produce intended and unintended results. Let's play this out with a simple example. My marketing experiences led to my belief in the power of mission. That belief led me to a set of actions:

» time devoted to building a mission in collaboration with my team, HR partners, and business leaders
» establishing mission-driven priorities
» funding and measuring priorities based on the mission.

The result of these actions was a mission-driven organization. Any organization embarking on a new strategy has to assess whether the current culture will work for or against the achievement of that strategy.

A great example of culture change in action happened in Yahoo! where we were driving a culture transformation that required teams to collaborate across boundaries to produce results. Nowhere was this more important than with our product and geography teams, two pivotal organizations that drove revenue. At the time, the experiences of the Asia Pacific (APAC) team were encapsulated in the belief that "The headquarters product team will never prioritize APAC and meet our unique needs. They can't be relied on to help us achieve our revenue goals and competitive position." Year after year, this belief had been formed based on a multitude of experiences. Their unique needs and functionality requirements were never prioritized on the product road map.

Based on this belief, they had a "localization team" that was really a shadow product development team. They built the products they needed and passively resisted any new product rollouts to their region. This worked to get them the products they needed. It didn't work when those products weren't part of the product road map and never got the ongoing support they needed from the engineering teams. And this meant Yahoo! was paying for two product generation teams with the same charter.

Going back to the model, the only way to change this situation was to change the APAC experience. How could we create a new belief that the product team in headquarters could actually help make great products for APAC? A new EVP of products came to the company, recognized this cultural problem, and began his APAC partnership by creating new experience that formed new beliefs. This is the power of culture transformation.

FIGURE 2-4. APAC Culture Change Applying the Results Pyramid

New Experiences	Create New Beliefs	Drives New Actions	Delivering Results
1. A new products executive video conferences with the APAC leadership to kick off a new partnership. The meeting is scheduled at 9 a.m. APAC time.	→ The new products executive cares about APAC. He didn't have a meeting with us at 2 a.m. our time!	→ APAC product leaders come to headquarters and are part of critical product development meetings.	→ Three-year global product road map with supported APAC features and products.
2. The products leadership team visits APAC and learns about local products. Together they decide on what gets integrated into the global road map.	→ The new products leadership team gets us and they party hard!	→ APAC products and critical functionality are on the new global product road map.	→ Achieve year one APAC required functionality.
3. The teams socialize, celebrating their new partnership.	→ The new products team has learned what APAC needs to be competitive in the region.	→ APAC products get the support they need.	→ APAC product position in the market is more competitive; they begin to take share from competitors.
4. An APAC product expert is assigned to every relevant product line.	→ We're part of a global team.	→ APAC participates in quarterly product reviews.	→ Collaborative leadership teams who communicate frequently, candidly share challenges, and celebrate successes.
5. Future APAC needs are prioritized into the global product road map.	→ We have partners in products we trust.	→ Headquarters teams participate in APAC business reviews in their countries.	

This model is also powerful for the L&TM teams I led. The only way to get them to believe we could be a key enabler for the business was to give them new experiences that would create this belief. I needed to shift the victim mentality of "I can only do what the business asks me to do" to a new belief that "I can be a powerful business partner who helps achieve business results." The new experiences of creating a powerful and clear business-focused mission, being embedded in the business structure, and having governance and sponsorship all fueled this new belief.

One Size Fits One

In closing, design and run your L&TM organization as an aligned system that supports and enables the larger business system. At the heart of this system is your culture, which will derail any efforts if it's ignored or misaligned with what you are trying to accomplish. Your organization must be healthy, running at high speed and on all cylinders to be relevant in today's volatile, uncertain, complex, and very ambiguous business environment. This chaotic business world will only get more challenging, and that will demand strong leadership and agile L&TM organizations. Are you ready?

3

Supercharging Your Learning Agenda Through Purpose, Culture, and Brand

Andrew Kilshaw

> In addition to focusing on the *what* of learning, learning leaders need to pay attention to the *how*—defining a learning purpose, creating a learning culture, and building a learning brand.

As learning leaders and practitioners, we often focus first and foremost on what our employees need to learn to build organizational capability that will deliver future success. Some of this focus is on generally timeless capabilities, such as supporting managerial and leadership transitions by applying current management and leadership theory. Other areas may be influenced by external political, socioeconomic, or technological forces that seek to disrupt business models—for example, adopting agile practices or leveraging AI through the value chain. Alternatively, it could include socioeconomic trends such as how to manage multiple generations in the workplace, or the emergence of the gig economy.

However, in addition to *what* we provide the learner, I would assert that the effectiveness of a company's learning agenda is equally influenced by *how* you design and deploy it.

Like any good company that competes for consumers' share of wallet knows, having great products is not enough. Increasingly, consumers and employees must feel a personal connection with a brand's or organization's purpose. We have more companies than ever with which we can choose to have relationships, and less discretionary time to do so, given today's fast-moving world.

A recent study by the Lovell Corporation (2017) of more than 2,000 respondents found that "for the first time, we see [Generation Z] prioritizing purpose in their work." It lists the top five work value priorities as:

1. interesting work
2. organization you're proud of
3. work you're passionate about
4. having the information to do your job
5. continuous learning.

Similarly important to clarity of organizational purpose, learning leaders can provide great value and build strategic learning organizations by stating their learning purpose: why learning is important for your employees and your organization. This provides a guiding star to define two further important aspects of learning that need to be aligned to the unique nature of your company: your learning culture and your learning brand.

The Evolving Role of the CLO

In the world of management science, there is a sizable body of work that highlights the importance of aligning your corporate culture with your purpose-led brand. After all, it is employees who, regardless of their function, ultimately deliver value for your customers or consumers. If employees are aligned both on what needs to be delivered (purpose and brand) and how they act individually and collectively (culture) in service of customers' needs, you have a positive recipe for a high-performing organization, especially in increasingly complex and evolving organizational structures.

Firstly, do you have a learning culture? Is your pedagogical philosophy tailored to the corporate culture and how people work? Secondly, do you have a learning brand that makes your learning portfolio accessible, consumable, and aligned with your company's brand and purpose?

During my time at IMD, one of the world's leading executive education providers, I was fortunate to deliver tailored executive education programs in partnership with several members of the Global Fortune 1000 list of companies. They spanned multiple industries, geographies, and corporate cultures, and I soon learned that each had uniquely tailored approaches to creating the best possible learning environment. The most effective companies focused on defining clear learning objectives, as you would expect. However, they equally ensured that pedagogy, learning branding, and accessibility worked best for their company's unique environment, and even acted as a mechanism to reinforce the corporate culture they aspired to.

Subsequently, I was able to study this in depth during my time as chief learning officer at two distinctly different companies (BlackRock and Nike), which have little in common other than being leaders in their respective industries. My team and I focused equally on balancing both building organizational capabilities and tailoring our design and deployment approach to the company culture. It's only when you do both well that you create what we all aspire to: a pull environment for employee development.

This approach is an evolution from the traditional view of a learning leader, who has a narrow but deep focus on employee development. It adds several dimensions that are more akin to the broader skill set of an enterprise general manager. Indeed, certain companies (such as Microsoft) have long adopted this thinking, referring to chief learning officers as GMs.

Through the rest of this chapter we will explore these concepts and their implications to ensure that purpose, culture, and brand are critical pillars of your organization's strategic plan for learning.

Defining the Purpose of the Learning Organization

In a world of greater transparency, net promoter scores, and democratized digital access to information, consumers and employees increasingly care deeply about a company's purpose. People are now accustomed to ask: Does it align with my priorities, my aspirations, and my personal values? Why should I choose, in a world of increasingly abundant options, to spend my money, align my personal brand, and dedicate my time to a relationship with this company?

Compounding this aspect of company existence, we live in a workplace with increased complexity, speed, and communications channels (or distractions). This creates more competition for your employees' "share of mind" and "share of calendar." Busier than ever, they need to understand why learning is of benefit to them personally, and how it is supportive of the company's success.

As Simon Sinek said in his TED talk, "Start with why." Specifically, you should assess why learning is important for your employees, your customers, and ultimately the company's success? By creating a learning purpose statement for your organization, you answer these questions and provide clear direction and parameters for your learning efforts, and subsequently how investments of both time and money are made.

A learning purpose statement might match a company's goals—for example, how a learner mindset versus a know-it-all mindset can help the radical transformation of companies facing disruption. Alternatively, you can take a very different angle. For example, at NikeU (Nike's corporate university) the U stood not for university but "Unleashing your potential," providing a distinctly personal and aspirational take on why learning is important within a competitive environment.

This elevator pitch also provides guidance to executives and the learning organization on why you exist, and importantly what is not your purpose. Such statements may be value-creating in nature, outlining the focus of future capabilities that will be developed to allow individuals and the company to grow. Purpose statements also may focus on reducing learning friction for the organization—NikeU was billed as "Nike's single destination for learning"—by making it easier for learners to find, access, and engage in employee development through personalized offerings.

Ultimately, organizations are made up of people, so learning leaders need to appeal to the "What's in it for me?" for employees on a personal level. This is especially important in a talent-constrained world with more career options and lower company tenure than ever. Employee development has long been a leading driver of engagement and retention, and it is more critical than ever—recent Gallup research (Rigoni and Nelson 2016) states that only 29 percent of Millennials are engaged with their jobs. Additionally, only 27 percent believe in their companies' values.

Creating a learning purpose statement engages employees and aligns and educates them on the personal and organizational benefits of being a continuous learner and the outcomes they should expect as a result. Executing this purpose in a manner that intentionally reinforces your culture, in practice and by example, should help increase both engagement and belief in a company's value.

What Is Organizational Culture?

The concept of what defines, and how to describe, organizational culture is its own voluminous body of work. For the purposes of this chapter I will define organizational culture as the total sum of the values, customs, traditions, and meanings that make an organization unique.

Often, a starting place to look for cultural descriptors is a company's set of values. This only gives a starting point however, as the following should also be considered:

» Do the organization's values, as stated, truly reflect the real customs and traditions that manifest day to day? Do they accurately describe the behavior of the vast majority of employees, or are they more aspirational? Enron's 2000 annual report listed communication, respect, integrity, and excellence. However, the company was regarded as a competitive, talent-focused culture where "stars" were lavishly rewarded, often without supervision.

» Are the corporate values uniform across the organization, or do they vary (significantly) by function or business unit? This can be tested by looking at the operational interdependence within the organization. Generally, more centralized organizations will exhibit more cultural homogeneity, versus more decentralized portfolio companies.

» For global organizations, to what extent does national culture outweigh corporate culture? For companies that have organically expanded geographically from a country headquarters, the prevailing culture may well be defined by that of the company's home nation. In companies formed from cross-border acquisitions, there may be more cultural dissonance reflecting the diversity of the merged organizations' native countries.

In addition to an organization's values, there are often other stated cultural artifacts, such as leadership principles, or expected behaviors that may be part of the "how" component of performance assessments.

How one measures culture may even be aligned with the culture itself. For example, Google, whose mission is "to organize the world's information and make it universally accessible and useful," is culturally highly data-driven. Google inherently takes a quantitative and empirical approach to defining an organization's characteristics as exemplified by Project Oxygen ("what makes a great manager?") and Project Aristotle ("what makes a team effective?").

On the other hand, Nike is well recognized for its storytelling, both as a brand to consumers and internally as a way of communicating purpose and behavior. In this instance, one might more effectively define culture by interviewing a representative cross-section of employees to solicit stories of how things get done. Alternatively, you could use metaphor, for example by asking, "If Nike were a person, how would you describe it?"

For your organization's culture, you might consider the Hagberg Consulting Group's five questions that get at the essence of a company's real culture (Inc. Staff n.d.):

» What 10 words would you use to describe your company?
» Around here, what's really important?
» Around here, who gets promoted?
» Around here, what behaviors get rewarded?
» Around here, who fits in and who doesn't?

To scale the qualitative collection process there are a large number of ever-changing tools that you can leverage (try googling "audience response software"). Many offer the ability to identify and distill trends, which can be presented through visuals such as word clouds.

Ultimately, a whole-brain approach that builds on and tests stated artifacts, through quantitative and qualitative engagement of employees, will give your team the most accurate description. Once you have an accurate understanding of your culture—in its current and potentially aspirational state (if different)—you can begin assessing the implications for your learning culture.

Creating a Supporting Learning Culture

Once you've developed a comprehensive understanding of your corporate culture, you can translate this to several aspects of your learning strategy.

This has two benefits. Firstly, you are making learning more consumable for employees, by making the act of learning in your company an aligned extension of "how we do things here." Secondly, it becomes a reinforcing mechanism of how workers are expected to behave, individually and collectively, whether it's "this is how we manage or lead here," or "this is how we work as Agile teams here." The required organizational capabilities may evolve, but there will be familiarity and reinforcement in the how.

For the sake of simplification, we will look at pedagogy through the lens of the 70-20-10 framework, which still underpins much learning design and is based on ongoing research at the Center for Creative Leadership, building on their original Lessons of Experience study (McCall, Lombardo, and Morrison 1988).

Applying Culture to Learning Through Experience (70 Percent)

The leading driver of leadership development is cited as providing challenging assignments through on-the-job experiences and challenges. Increasingly, this is true also for developing all employees, and is as much about macro experiences as it is about microlearning in the flow of work.

As organizational leaders and managers create intentional learning experiences for employees, they should consider cultural guideposts. Table 3-1 looks at contrasting dimensions of culture and how that might influence learning experience design.

TABLE 3-1. Culture and Learning Through Experience

Highly Regulated, With Low Risk Tolerance	Inventive, Disruptive, and Innovative
Heavier governance and oversight of experiences; low cost of failure; multiple go and no-go checkpoints	Less governance or oversight and self-regulated; high value in failure; iterative and Agile with ability to pivot and repurpose
Academic and Led With Intellect	**Results Orientation: "Just Do It"**
Moments for intellectual reflection on real-world derived theoretical models; reflective journaling	Agile sprints and tangible pilot-driven prototyping; creating and testing to iteratively refine through experience
Individualistic Achievement Culture	**Collaborative Group Achievement Culture**
Individually led experiential learning through individual projects that promote personal growth	Leaderless self-led group action learning, with implied organizational ambiguity and collective ownership of learning experience outcomes

Applying Culture to Learning From Others (20 Percent)

Developmental relationships play a key part in developing an organization's employees, particularly its leaders, with key relationships being with managers, between peers, and formal mentors and coaches. Cultural preferences may steer your focus on which relationships are most successful. Table 3-2 presents the spectrum of cultural influence in learning from others.

TABLE 3-2. Culture and Learning From Others

Management and Leadership Capability Valued Over Technical Acumen	Technical Acumen Valued Over Management Capability
Managers are equipped, assessed, and rewarded to provide coaching and feedback to their teams, through informal discussion and formal feedback processes	While managers are trained and expected to provide direct feedback and coaching, internally or externally trained professional coaches augment the learners' access to 20 percent learning
Academic and Led With Intellect	**Results Orientation: "Just Do It"**
Conversations tend to be Socratic, with reflective theoretical "what if" discussions around actions and consequences	After-action debriefs occur around observed behavior and results, and future action plans to refine behavior are discussed and implemented
Growth Contained by Departmental Silos With Limited Cross-Functional Collaboration	**Cross-Functional Growth With Highly Matrixed Collaboration**
Coaches and mentors are functionally expert, with learning coming from growth discussions within functional boundaries	Coaches and mentors are intentionally multi-functional and focus more on enterprise collaboration and organizational navigation and being able to walk in the shoes of other functions

Applying Culture to Formal Learning (10 Percent)

While formal learning from courses forms the smallest component of a blended learning approach, it is still an important part of knowledge transfer, which can then be applied through practice and feedback from others. Given the proliferation of learning technologies, there are a multitude of modes of formal learning that can be tailored according to the organization's predominant culture (Table 3-3).

TABLE 3-3. Culture and Formal Learning

Specialized Company With Internal Focus	Connected Company and More Externally Focused
Generates internal case studies that tell stories of the past and highlight successes and failures from within the organization (Apple was famous for doing this)	Outside-in learning, through speakers and external case studies; consider mixing cross-functional and cross-company cohorts through open enrollment programs
Academic and Led With Intellect	**Results Orientation: "Just Do It"**
Uses academic research and case studies, with hypothetical exploration (in either self or group study) to explore likely scenarios	Provides basic concepts to be practiced through individual or collective simulations, with real feedback loops to learn from consequences of actions
Growth Contained by Departmental Silos With Limited Cross-Functional Collaboration	**Cross-Functional Growth With Highly Matrixed Cross-Functional Collaboration**
Coaches and mentors are functionally expert, with learning coming from growth discussions within functional boundaries	Coaches and mentors are intentionally multi-functional and focus more on enterprise collaboration and organizational navigation and being able to "walk in the shoes" of other functions

As we consider learning cultures, which are collective in nature, we should make sure we do not confuse this with learning styles, which are more individualistic. Learning styles are competing theories that propose differing preferences in consumption of learning.

One popular theory, known as the VARK model, was developed by Neil Fleming after his observations of classroom effectiveness while working as a school inspector in New Zealand. Fleming proposed that learners have preferred learning experiences. VARK stands for Visual, Auditory, Reading, and Kinesthetic learning styles, and Fleming devised a questionnaire to help individuals identify their personal preferences. It should be noted that multiple studies have debunked the correlation between learning styles and effectiveness. In the same manner, it should be noted that while organizational cultures are collectively predominant but do not make us clones on an individual level, the same can be said around learning culture.

This thinking equally applies to organizational learning. While there may be predominant types of learning programs that work more effectively across the preceding categories, strategic learning organizations should provide enough options and flexibility so learners can customize most effectively to their learning preferences.

Building a Learning Brand

Once you have defined your learning purpose and culture, you can then build out an aligned curriculum and set of learning assets using learning techniques that reinforce "how we do things here."

However, we know that companies cannot rely only on a great consumer-centered product portfolio alone. It takes clear brand messaging that resonates with consumers, and a go-to-market distribution strategy that gets great products in their hands to fully execute a strategy. This is no different for a learning function that is vying against the multiple competing priorities of employees.

During my transition from BlackRock to Nike in 2010, I moved between two very different industries, business models, and brands. As an avid consumer of Nike, who was very aware of their storytelling success, that wasn't a surprise to me. What was a surprise, however, was the extent to which leaders similarly used the power of storytelling, visual aesthetic, and a message of unlimited potential with employees.

Within the first three months of being at Nike, as someone with limited prior marketing exposure, I realized I was out of my depth. Fortunately, to quote one of Nike's founders, Bill Bowerman, "Everything you need is already inside." In this case, we had access to some of the best marketing talent in the world, and we invited a marketing executive to address the leadership team on how to build a brand for our learning organization. That began a journey, which saw us partner with an external brand agency to define how we wanted to show up, what language we would use, and how we'd communicate our purpose to executives and, most importantly, to employees.

What was born was NikeU, an aspirational learning brand. It was the basis for how we talked about learning. At BlackRock, the U would have indeed stood for university, given the high number of academics with post-graduate degrees. At Nike it stood for Us, YoU, Unleashing our collective potential, Unlimited opportunities, Unconventional success.

Knowing that visual aesthetic was important, we developed the visual brand to serve as the basis for all our materials. That included a custom-built LMS, using Moodle and Drupal, the only platforms at the time that would support the design aesthetic and media capability we needed to distribute learning globally. You can see the trailer for NikeU on YouTube.

Combining Your Brand With a Go-to-Market Strategy

Both a great product set and a brand need one final step to reach the consumer: a comprehensive and tailored go-to-market strategy.

This is not a typical capability within a learning function. At Nike we believed this to be a highly important one, so we created a role whose sole purpose was about go-to-market—creating channels to get learning in the hands of employees.

Using a well-known sales and marketing approach—the AIDAR model (Figure 3-1)—we mapped activities that we could take to drive learner engagement using a branded approach that would communicate well with a Nike employee. Table 3-4 summarizes some of these activities.

FIGURE 3-1. The AIDAR Model

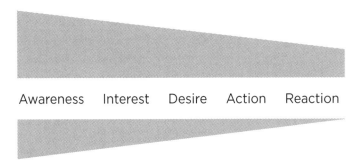

Awareness   Interest   Desire   Action   Reaction

TABLE 3-4. AIDAR Marketing Strategies at Nike

Awareness	Interest	Desire	Action	Reaction
• Creation of a recognizable learning brand • Digital and in-office promotion • Leadership team cascades	• Use of Nike lexicon and communication style • Peer-to-peer verbatim program feedback and Yelp-like star ratings for all programs	• Senior-level sponsorship and involvement in learning programs • Identification of internal learning influencer advocates	• Creation of localized offerings that can be accessed online or in person • Removal of friction for learners to learn	• Gamification and leaderboards to encourage recognition and competition • Recognition of learning leaders, promoting their stories through internal communications

Leveraging Other Marketing Best Practices

Lastly, when you empathize with the learner and design for service on their terms, you realize there are two key innovations that make their lives easier and remove friction from the learning process: personalization and feedback.

Personalization

Great learning organizations are strategic and purposeful in creation of content, but in my opinion they should be agnostic on distribution of content. In today's world, it can be even easier to learn on-demand from Google, Wikipedia, podcasts, and TED talks than it is to access internally created content.

One key way of removing friction for the consumer is to be a master aggregator—or what we at Nike called "being the Amazon.com of learning." This means that from the perspective of the learner, you are agnostic on the origins of content. You just need to believe it's reputable, credible, and relevant to the skills gap you're trying to close. We sought to harvest and merchandize learning content into three buckets:

» **Must-own content:** This is the content we believed important to own the design, development, and delivery of. For Amazon, that's Alexa devices or the Kindle. Those are critical to their operations. At Nike that was management and leadership development and onboarding; these aren't things that necessarily should be decentralized, as they affect to the business at its core, and align to principles and competencies that HR generally owns.

» **Functional content:** This is content where we bring our expertise in instructional design and apply it to functional experts' knowledge (and budget). For Amazon, this is where they apply their online e-commerce expertise to electronics, books, and other categories. They aren't writing or publishing books, but they are expert retailers of these products. The learning team at Nike wasn't full of experts in merchandising or sales, but we knew how to create great learning programs on that content.

- » **Commodity content:** This is typically off-the-shelf, plug-and-play content, such as Excel training, or a quick course on how to use the expense system. For Amazon, it's their marketplace, where they provide a platform for third-party resellers to reach consumers.

Ultimately, we wanted to be the one-stop shop for learning at Nike, irrespective of the origin of the content. As Amazon knows, consumers don't care—they just want to find what they need and get it easily. Employees want the same frictionless experience in accessing learning, and creating sortable databases that filter via tagged content (such as location, topic, learning level, and so on) is a smart way of doing this.

With the addition of machine learning and AI, it's getting easier to do this. High-growth learning providers, such as Degreed and OpenSesame, are creating a new category in learning content aggregation: delivering learner-right assortments of content that are personalized to you, how you need it, when you need it. Learn to curate content as well as create.

Feedback

In times of increased transparency and first-party generated public feedback, I believe the same should apply to learning. For example, when booking accommodation, you know what people thought of an Airbnb by the reviews prior guests have left. You know what your Uber driver is known for before you get in their car.

Gone are the days of feedback paper questionnaires at the end of a class session. The learner journey with any interaction with a learning product should end in open, public, and frank feedback that other learners can take into account when choosing their learning.

At Nike, we observed three benefits of this approach.
- » Learners are more credible than the learning function when talking to their peers about the applicability of the development experience. They can convey the value of the learning in language that better resonates with their colleagues, helping learners choose the right content.
- » It creates a sense of trust with employees, in both the transparency of the learning function and its desire to learn from feedback and strive for improved quality of content and delivery.
- » It creates true accountability to act on behalf of the learning team. As an Airbnb host, I want as many five-star reviews as possible, and I listen closely to feedback to ensure I am giving a service that our guests want. The same is true for those who own the design and delivery of learning solutions for employees. While the transition to this level of transparency can be hard and at times painful if feedback isn't complimentary, it clears the path between instructor and learner to truly listen, learn, and respond to the needs of employees.

This feedback process creates sources of fantastic data that allow you to evolve learning portfolios, pedagogical approaches, and even logistical improvements. It creates an opportunity for greater learner empathy, by which you can improve your offerings.

Closing Advice

In opening this chapter, I suggested that the modern role of the CLO and their team is less that of solely being a learning function expert, and more akin to being an enterprise general manager. In addition to focusing on the what of learning, learning leaders need to pay attention to the how—defining the purpose of learning, creating a learning culture, and building a learning brand.

The good news, as evidenced by some of my examples, is it's increasingly possible for learning leaders to master the primary skill sets they need to be learning GMs, whether it's looking to those who've mastered technology in creating personalized assortments of products, such as Amazon or Degreed, or leveraging your relationship with your CMO. In the words of Interbrand, "There has never been a better opportunity for HR and marketing to become the best of friends."

Lastly, by learning and mastering a broader set of skills, it allows us to have greater appreciation of, and increased credibility with those we all seek to serve: the organization's employee population.

4

The Five Building Blocks of a Learning Ecosystem

Marina Theodotou

> Learning boosts performance and drives productivity. Creating a learning ecosystem requires a focus on the people, content, technology, data, and governance in the organization.

Today, like never before in human history, digitization, automation, and acceleration in the business world are transforming learning and emphasizing new essential skills employees need to have for survival—both their own and that of their organization. Darwin's maxim on the survival of the fittest has never rung louder in the business world: Companies that do not reskill and upskill their employees will not survive. The *2018 Company Longevity Forecast* reports that longevity for S&P 500 companies has shrunk from an average of 33 years in 1964 to 24 years in 2016, to a forecasted 12 years by 2027. This decrease in company longevity means that more than 50 percent of all S&P 500 companies will not survive through the 2020s. Companies that want to survive must continually reskill and sustainably upskill their employees. But such a reskilling scenario is not easy. To upskill and reskill efficiently and effectively, organizations must build a learning ecosystem.

In this chapter, I'll discuss what a learning ecosystem is and why learning leaders should care if they want to create a strategic learning organization. I'll share the essential building blocks for creating a learning ecosystem. Next, I'll analyze the three phases of the learning ecosystem life cycle so you can plan and gauge where you are. Then, I'll provide tried and tested tips to build a culture of learning that holds your learning ecosystem together. Finally, I will share two use cases to answer the questions "What does a learning ecosystem look like in real life?" and "What are some use cases of organizations that built a successful ecosystem?" Let's get started!

What Is a Learning Ecosystem, and Why Should You Care?

A learning ecosystem is a symbiotic environment where people interact with the content, technologies, and data that surround them to facilitate and deliver learning experiences based on the governance guardrails set by the organization. These elements comprise the five basic building blocks to a learning ecosystem: people, content, technology, data, and governance, which I'll discuss in the following section in more detail. A learning ecosystem can be broad and organization-agnostic, open and accessible to anyone (think of LinkedIn and how much you learn, connect, and engage with other professionals daily), or specific and organization-centric (existing within your organization). The resilience and survival of the ecosystem depend on the variety and diversity of the people and content in it, as well as the frequency, ease, and depth of the interaction facilitated by the underlying technologies. Here, let's focus on organization-specific learning ecosystems, which are more thoroughly within your control.

Organization-specific ecosystems that embrace a diversity of content, access, and types of learning foster innovation and are more resilient to change than closed and rigid systems. A poignant example of an organizational ecosystem that was not permeable and did not embrace new ideas, learning, and innovation is the rise and demise of Kodak. In 1975, Steven Sasson, a 24-year-old engineer, created a camera that took photos and recorded them on cassette tapes that were then displayed on a TV screen. Instead of using the invention as a new product to learn about customer needs and evolve current product offerings, Kodak executives buried the digital camera (Lucas and Goh 2009). They could not see the value of viewing photos on a screen rather than printing on paper. Of course, we know how the story ends: In 2012, Eastman Kodak filed for bankruptcy and lost its market dominance in the U.S. photo market forever. While several other business drivers converged to drive Kodak's fall, from an L&D perspective, the lesson learned from Kodak is twofold: First, it is crucial to foster a permeable instead of rigid learning ecosystem, and second, it is vital to encourage and welcome creativity and innovation in that ecosystem.

Kodak's and other similar companies' decline should offer an easy answer to why you should care about building a learning ecosystem. But let's examine it more thoroughly. As an L&D leader you should care for three reasons: to increase employee engagement, cut reskilling costs, and improve innovation and performance in your organization.

With digitization and artificial intelligence (AI) reshaping the way we do business and the way we learn, one of the most effective ways L&D can help employees keep up with this exponential change is by creating and fostering a learning ecosystem that provides engaging and meaningful learning experiences. According to Gallup, when employees feel supported by their organization to grow and learn, they are more engaged. Gallup defines 12 key employee engagement elements that link to improved business outcomes. These 12 elements relate to four interactions between the employee and the organization:

» what the employee gets from the organization
» what the employee gives back to the organization
» whether the employee fits in the organization
» whether the employee has an opportunity to grow in the organization.

This last interaction centers on whether the organization has a learning ecosystem to support and enable the employee to grow. With a vibrant learning ecosystem, you can decrease the cost of an unengaged employee, which, according to LinkedIn, can be as high as $50,000 per employee per year.

Additionally, with a learning ecosystem, you can curtail reskilling costs, which *The Future of Jobs* report published by the World Economic Forum (2019) estimated to be $24,800 per employee. The same report estimated that 1.37 million employees will require reskilling during this decade, escalating costs to $34 billion, which is no small chunk of change and will affect all organizations. The L&D function can conduct a gap analysis of the skills needed, the skills available, and the number of employees who will require reskilling in the organization to calculate the costs. Learning leaders are first in line for responsibility to champion reskilling employees in their organizations.

Lastly, learning ecosystems encourage collective curiosity and innovation in employees, which in turn improves performance. In his 2019 TEDxDAU talk, Josh Smith, director of the Tactical Advancements for the Next Generation (TANG), a design thinking initiative for the US Navy at the Johns Hopkins Applied Physics Lab, provides a successful use case of TANG fostering a learning ecosystem and producing new solutions for sailors and submariners, including a Microsoft X-Box inspired submarine periscope controller. In the same talk, Smith references research from Harvard professor Francesca Gino that shows that promoting collectively curious teams can improve outcomes and performance. Learning leaders must promote learning ecosystems that inspire curiosity, creativity, and innovation. Not only must you care about learning ecosystems, but you also have a responsibility to build, nurture, and cultivate them.

What Are the Building Blocks of a Learning Ecosystem?

The five building blocks of a learning ecosystem are people, content, technology, data, and governance. Let's examine each.

People

The main beneficiaries of your organization's learning ecosystem are its employees, but the quality and depth the ecosystem in turn benefits your customers. The better your employees learn through the ecosystem, the better the quality of the products and services they will provide to your customers. The ecosystem may include other stakeholders such as university faculty, professional association members, policymakers, and other industry vendors that your employees engage with during their learning journeys.

Content

The content in the ecosystem includes the learning courses your organization offers, from classroom instructor-led to online courses, videos, articles, podcasts, on-the-job tools, guides, e-books, webcasts, and webinars. Content curation is critical here because it will enable you to address the needs of your learners.

Technology

As of the writing of this chapter, the most viable technology to support and foster a learning ecosystem is a learning experience platform (LXP), which is increasingly replacing the traditional learning management system (LMS). Bersin by Deloitte defines a learning experience platform as "a single-point access, consumer-grade system composed of integrated technologies for enabling learning. An LXP can curate and aggregate content, create learning and career pathways, enable networking, enhance skill development, and track multiple learning activities delivered by multiple channels and content partners" (Bersin 2018). LXPs provide detailed data, empowering the learner to track and own their learning journey and the employer to make talent management and retention decisions for the organization.

Data

Data is critical for your ecosystem because it will help you analyze the behaviors of your employees. Through the data you can collect from your underlying ecosystem technology platform, you can learn more about how, when, and where your employees like to learn. You can track which type of content and modality your employees prefer. Based on the data on learner preferences, you can make decisions about which learning assets to keep, which to expand upon, and which to eliminate.

Governance

A key concern when it comes to governance is balancing the need for centralized coordination of the various ecosystem elements with the flexibility to allow the ecosystem to grow organically. You and your team will have to address several questions relating to the ecosystem members, the content, the technologies, and the processes within the context, mission, vision, and strategy of your organization. For example, who can join the ecosystem? How will the content be provided to the learners? How often will it be refreshed? How will the ecosystem evolve? What data will be collected, and why? How will content be released to various groups? Will the ecosystem include communities of practice? How will they be organized? Once you have defined and answered the key governance questions, you can announce the establishment of your ecosystem.

In addition to these building blocks, you will need to consider the three phases of the learning ecosystem life cycle so you and your team can be prepared to manage the challenges of each before progressing to the next.

What Is the Learning Ecosystem Life Cycle, and Which Phase Are You In?

The learning ecosystem life cycle is an adaptation of the Global Startup Ecosystem model, which illustrates the life cycle for start-ups. In the learning context, the learning ecosystem life cycle has three phases: activation, adoption, and integration. Each phase has its own characteristics, challenges, objectives, and metrics. You can use this life cycle to gauge the progress and maturity of your learning ecosystem. Figure 4-1 depicts the three phases based on the law of diffusion of innovation defined by Everett Rogers in 1962.

FIGURE 4-1. Diffusion of Innovation for a Learning Ecosystem

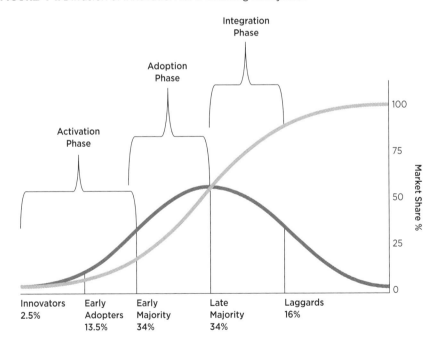

Activation Phase

The first phase of the learning ecosystem cycle is characterized by the limited number of players, a low number of learning assets and experiences developed and used, and the small number of exchanges in information and learning. Challenges you may face when getting a learning ecosystem started include a lack of trust from employees in the ecosystem and not enough users to encourage others to participate.

The goal of this phase is to reach the tipping point at 16 percent (the 2.5 percent of the total who represent innovators, plus the 13.5 percent who are early adopters), as seen in Figure 4-1. Based on my analysis and experience at my last three organizations, this may take between three and six months to reach, depending on the number of employees in the organization.

In this phase, focus on increasing user engagement by highlighting the positive experiences of those already engaged, the innovators and early adopters. Enable them to share and connect with other employees about their experiences using the ecosystem. Pick a handful of innovators and feature them in videos, blog posts, and podcasts within your company's social media space to discuss their experience and the value added to their personal and professional growth as a result of engaging in the ecosystem. This will help you increase awareness about the ecosystem and underscore what it offers to employees.

Adoption Phase

The second phase is when a critical mass of employees in your organization opt to participate in the learning ecosystem. To get here, you'll have to increase the number of learning assets and experiences developed. As a result, you'll start to see a greater number of exchanges in information and learning programs. Getting to the necessary adoption phase will likely take longer than starting the ecosystem in the first place; perhaps between six and 18 months. And unlike the graph in Figure 4-1, the adoption rate might not always slope upward; you may face periods of rapid adoption followed by declining engagement.

During this phase, you must focus on significantly expanding the number of members to the ecosystem until you reach 50 percent of your organization (the 34 percent who represent the early majority, in addition to the innovators and early adopters). There are several ways to do this; I recommend a three-pronged strategy of communication, curation, and consistency. You can start by developing and implementing a robust, relatable, and engaging communications strategy on any of your organization's internal channels (intranet, workplace social media, email) to highlight the value the learning ecosystem brings to individual career growth and the benefits to the organization.

You also need to focus on content curation. To ensure your organization continues to use and value the learning ecosystem, you must close any quality or relevancy gaps in the learning assets that might have lingered during the activation phase. You can turn to reviewing learning experience related analytics and leveraging the content curation or AI and machine learning capabilities in your underlying learning experience platform.

Last, you must get serious on consistency; are learning assets and events available daily, weekly, or monthly? Are you consistent in your communication of new learning experiences? Are you continually curating new content? During this phase, you also may want to engage additional resources to help you scale as you progress to the next and final phase of the learning ecosystem life cycle, integration.

Integration Phase

The third phase means you've been able to reach about 75 percent of all employees in your organization, with more learning assets developed and being used and a large number of exchanges in information and learning occurring daily, weekly, and monthly. Similar to the adoption phase, you'll need to manage attrition of early adopters and maintain the number of the late majority by ensuring the quality of the learning experience. For smaller organizations this can take six months, but for larger organizations, reaching the late majority can take up to 18 months.

In this phase, it is essential to improve the quality and freshness of content. Does it meet the needs of the learners whenever and wherever they want to learn? Does the learning ecosystem offer a wide variety of learning experiences and events to appeal to different preferences of the learners? You must ensure you are continuously monitoring learner preferences so you can update the learning experiences to meet their needs.

To sustain the ecosystem and beyond, your focus must evolve to cultivating further the culture of learning in your organization so learning becomes integrated into every business line, product, and service your organization offers—to the point where interacting with the ecosystem becomes embedded in the daily actions of employees intuitively and naturally, rather than being a forced experience. The culture of learning will serve as the binding force that ties your learning ecosystem to the organization and its strategy.

A Culture of Learning: The Oxygen for a Learning Ecosystem

If organizational strategy represents the plans, goals, and metrics of how to organize people to reach a goal, then culture is people. The way an organization deals with problems and the way it learns (or doesn't) from these problems depends on the culture of learning in the organization. Organizations that want to engage their talent and drive for results to increase performance must focus on building an enduring culture of learning, one that aligns the learning programs they offer to their C-suite business performance results. A culture of learning becomes the oxygen that enables the learning ecosystem to breathe and then flourish by allowing the people to interact with the content, technologies, data, and governance of that ecosystem.

This is easier said than done.

And that is why I have focused on it during my career. Using the Clark & Estes Knowledge, Motivation, and Organizational Influences model, I have distilled three actionable and practical steps to help learning leaders and their teams build an enduring learning culture that aligns their learning to business performance results:

» foster confidence, creativity, and commitment in your team
» align metrics, strategy, and resources to the CEO agenda
» cultivate continuous improvement.

Here is what my experience and research has revealed.

Step 1: Foster Confidence, Creativity, and Commitment in Your L&D Team

This step can be broken down into several actions.

Start With "Why"

As Simon Sinek recommends, before embarking on an organizational change effort, the company must start at the beginning to ensure that everyone is on board with the why. To do this, you can conduct brainstorming and training sessions to empower and enable your teams to define their organizational values (their why).

Encourage Innovative and Creative Problem Solving

Empower your teams to think innovatively and creatively through design thinking and Agile training sessions. These sessions will help L&D teams increase efficiencies, develop new ideas, and become empowered to embrace their own notions of choice and control over these ideas through specific tasks and activities to implement them.

Communicate Openly

This begins with you and cascades to your senior L&D managers all the way to the individual team members. Openness means that the team communicates about successes and challenges alike. Communication can be expressed verbally, in writing, and nonverbally.

Hire, Develop, and Retain Great People

You and your L&D management team, using the values defined by the why, must establish a talent acquisition, development, and retention plan centering on hiring the right people for both the L&D team and your organization as a whole, providing them with learning opportunities that are recognized with specific rewards and programs that foster work and life balance.

Step 2: Align Metrics, Strategy, and Resources to the CEO Agenda

Let's take a look at how this step breaks down.

Collect the Right Data

Engage the L&D team with the C-suite through consistent, periodic meetings with organizational leaders to listen to their vision and provide insight on how to implement it through the learning strategy. From these meetings, draft a data collection plan to ensure that the team is collecting the right data, and set metrics that align with the vital C-suite goals.

Develop a Strategic Plan

Your L&D team will need to develop a strategy for the whole organization. Provide your team training sessions and tools on how to develop a strategy, how to conduct an environmental scan externally of the industry and internally of the organization, how to do a SWOT analysis, and how to set SMART goals. The data from these components and the budget will be used to build the strategic plan.

Align Your Resources to the CEO's Agenda

Having set the metrics and the strategic plan, you and your L&D management team must align the budget, the people, and the technology resources to the organizational priorities gleaned from the meetings with the C-suite to ensure that all align to the CEO agenda.

Step 3: Cultivate Continuous Improvement

These actions will help you reap the benefits of what you've created in a sustained way.

Benchmark the Best

Provide learning resources and training to the L&D team so they can learn how to conduct benchmarking, identify best practice organizations within and outside their industry, and engage in visits to collect, glean, adopt, and adapt best practices within the learning and development division and the organization as a whole.

Seek Accreditation

This step pertains to corporate universities. You can provide guidance and learning opportunities to the L&D team to prepare, seek, and obtain higher educational institution accreditation from organizations such as the Council for Opportunity in Education and Distance Education Accrediting Commission.

Apply for Industry Awards

Similar to accreditation, L&D teams can apply for industry awards such as ATD's BEST or Excellence in Practice awards, the *Chief Learning Officer* LearningElite award, Brandon Hall, and Training Industry. In this case, you and your team will need to commit to the rigorous application preparation, submission, and communication process required by such awards.

Building Learning Ecosystems: Two Successful Use Cases

Now let's explore two use cases of these concepts.

"Would you buy a car with the hood welded shut?" (Red Hat)

This question, and "How much do you know about modern internal combustion engines?" are two questions Red Hat co-founder Bo Young would ask in his business development meetings a few years ago when discussing their decision to build an open-source cloud software ecosystem.

Red Hat is an open-source cloud technology company that built a fast-moving ecosystem of innovation. By listening to its customers and observing their needs, Red Hat identified a need and lack of response in the market: Businesses using off-the-shelf software to build their technology infrastructure to sell their goods and services was similar to buying a car with the hood welded shut. This limitation resulted in high costs and unmet customer needs. Specifically, Red Hat observed that the boxed-software vendors overcharged their customers, refused or took too long to fix the software bugs reported, and often did not release the features customers needed. Red Hat began operations as a start-up in the early 2000s, and, to address the customer's unmet needs, decided to share all the software technology they created in an open-source environment.

Essentially, Red Hat's success lies in building a learning ecosystem for its customers. To do that, the company first built a learning ecosystem for its employees. A closer study of Red Hat reveals that they implemented at least four of the best practices identified in this chapter.

They Started With "Why"

In 2009, Red Hat leadership realized that they had to develop a crisp and concise statement describing why they existed (Red Hat n.d.). They brought together more than 400 Red Hat employees and together crafted the mission statement, which reads: "To be the catalyst in communities of customers, contributors, and partners creating better technology the open source way."

They Communicated Openly

According to Red Hat, employees "were free to say anything they liked, both in meetings and on the company wide email list." Open communication implied both empowerment and accountability: empowerment to voice one's perspective and the accountability to back it up with merit and data.

They Encouraged Employees to Think Innovatively and Be Creative in Problem Solving

Red Hat, like every organization, faced intense market pressures due to the complexity and velocity of change. Throughout this journey, they encouraged their employees to continue applying open source principles to experiment, ideate, prototype, and innovate. Red Hat cultivated "pragmatic renewal" by allowing its employees to continuously innovate.

They Aligned With the CEO's Agenda

The decision to make their product open source was taken at the CEO level. Employees aligned with the CEO agenda and were empowered to think innovatively.

As a result, Red Hat created Fedora, a freely available, open, cloud-based operating system, through rapid iterations and experimentation with their customers. Today, Red Hat collaborates with thousands of contributors who code in Fedora and keep it free. In the summer of 2019, Red Hat was acquired by IBM for $34 billion (Red Hat 2019).

Shifting Focus on the Learner: Caterpillar

Caterpillar is a Fortune 500 company that manufactures and sells machinery, financial products, and insurance through 172 dealers worldwide. Their compliance content for dealers was product focused. Learners at their 172 dealerships found the content time-consuming, dense, daunting, and difficult to absorb and apply.

The Caterpillar director of global dealer learning and his L&D team decided to shift the focus to the learners and their needs. To build a learner-focused learning ecosystem, Caterpillar implemented three best practices from the enduring culture of learning model discussed in this chapter.

They Collected the Right Data

The L&D team started collecting data relating to how the learners where engaging with the content, for how long, what paths they followed to access the content, and which videos they viewed fully versus dropping off before the video even reached halfway. By collecting and analyzing the right data, Caterpillar was able to gain valuable insights about learner needs and behaviors.

They Developed a Strategic Plan

Based on the data they collected on learner preferences and needs, Caterpillar was now able to create new learning content that aligned with those needs, such as shorter videos, crisper articles, and more concise learning modules. The L&D team created a strategy for learning content development that prioritized the needs of the learner.

They Aligned With the CEO and Organizational Strategy

With meaningful data on learner preferences at hand and a strategy on how to develop such learning, the L&D team also defined learning metrics that aligned with the CEO's organizational key performance indicators (KPIs). By delving into the learner data collected, the L&D team can tie the results back to the KPIs to detect how the learning strategy aligns with organizational performance.

As a result of all these efforts, Caterpillar learners in 172 countries now have access to learning assets that are better aligned with their needs and preferences (Watershed Systems 2019). Additionally, Caterpillar enables learners to create their own learning assets, such as videos on topics of subject matter expertise, transforming the learner from consumer to creator in a virtuous and continuous circle of learning.

Charting Your Learning Ecosystem Journey

Building and cultivating a learning ecosystem in your organization is not something you can achieve easily, quickly, or too cheaply. As a learning leader, you will need to consider the end state: why your organization needs a learning ecosystem; how it will impact your employees, your customers, and your stakeholders; and which building blocks you will use to build it. You need to consider content that is dynamic and shareable and a technology that can evolve with the needs of your learners. You also must develop a culture of learning to keep the ecosystem growing. You need to define relevant metrics to track your progress along the learning ecosystem life cycle, and you will benefit from examining other use cases for possible lessons learned.

You are now ready to embark on your learning ecosystem journey. Good luck!

5

Winning at Shark Tank: How L&D Leaders Really Gain Management Support

Kevin D. Wilde

> Learning leader success is less about settling into a seat at the table and more about winning your *Shark Tank* appointment with organizational stakeholders.

Conference sessions, blog posts, webcasts. You're likely to see the same "seat at the table" dilemma facing leaders of learning and development departments with similar solutions. But garnering line management support for your L&D initiative is more akin to walking onto the set of the popular TV show *Shark Tank*, where budding entrepreneurs meet a panel of skeptical investors to explain their idea and win an investment. The stage lights are bright, the camera is recording your every move, and you have about 90 seconds to catch their attention. The long-running TV show speaks to the reality of winning support for a worthy L&D idea. It won't succeed without real support from line managers and executives.

First, recognize that the shark investors (your organization's senior leaders and managers) couldn't care less about winning learning organization awards. If you're imagining yourself on stage accepting an L&D trophy and returning to the office to thunderous applause, you probably should skip this chapter. On the other hand, if you see yourself doing great work that helps your organization and the managers win, read on. The sharks want to hear what you have to say.

Second, the sharks have a lot on their minds and your idea swims in a sea of good ideas being pitched to them. They likely just heard from marketing about a new investment proposal and after you it's operations, customer service, and legal teams waiting in the wings. All proposals pitch themselves as exciting, innovative, and requiring a consequential investment of time and money. But resources are limited, and attention is fleeting. You better be at your best.

Third, gaining support isn't a set of secrets, but more about doing the things commonly talked about but rarely practiced well or consistently. The trap is often getting too excited about a new L&D idea and forgetting what you know about strategic influence. You cut corners when striving to be influential, convinced the payoff is obvious and your time is better spent managing L&D. As a result, the great L&D idea goes unfunded as one shark after another declares, "I'm out."

I know that sinking feeling; I've experienced it more times that I care to admit. And yes, I've at times forgotten lessons learned about the best way to secure support. But I've also been fortunate to work with great L&D teams where we've secured the deal, delivering strong value-add contributions to business success. And in the end, the work was noticed by others, winning awards over the years such as #1 Learning Elite Organization, Best Company for Leaders, Training Top Company, and CLO of the year. My sharks provided outstanding commitment too, but it wasn't in pursuit of the L&D profession accolades. They supported L&D because it was delivering what mattered to them.

So how do you win in the shark tank of management support? The following four principles are the result of a series of interviews with outstanding L&D executives, most with a trophy case full of awards but more importantly recognition from their leaders as critical must-have partners for business success. Also included are insights from savvy external learning providers who have worked with hundreds of L&D leaders worldwide.

Principle 1: Proactively Build Strong Partner Relationships

If you've ever binge watched *Shark Tank*, you'll start to see patterns emerge that you'd miss by only viewing one episode. In particular, you'll pick up on a common set of favorite questions each investor shark likes to ask. One will often inquire about the pricing model and cash flow, trying to figure out the long-term profitability potential. Others have favorite lines of inquiry about exclusivity or threat of competition, distribution potential, and scaling capabilities. All are sizing up the competence and collaborative bent of the entrepreneur.

Now, imagine as an L&D leader you are facing your internal senior management sharks to gain commitment and support for your great learning initiative. The inquiring panel might include the CFO; the heads of marketing, sales, and operations; and major business or regional leaders. In any one encounter, their questions will sound fresh and spontaneous to you. But like the hosts of the TV show, each of your business sharks have their own interests, points of view, and favorite questions to weigh business proposals. For example, your sales leader defaults to two considerations: What's the time commitment that would take front-line sales reps away from customers as they learn, and how quickly will revenue increase from these educated sales reps? The more you know about their prime interests, the better you can craft L&D ideas that match their thinking and concerns and the better you can entice them by competently addressing their motives and concerns.

This starts with not assuming the self-evident brilliance of your L&D proposal will win the day. You'll need to pitch well. Sharks can miss great ideas. In 2013, *Shark Tank* passed on investing in Ring—a doorbell and video camera that connects to smartphones. Amazon later bought Ring for more than $1 billion. So you need to invest your time and energy to connect with these leaders or stakeholders and learn their interests before you take the stage and pitch your L&D initiative. That's the point of building relationships and partnerships upfront.

How To

If anyone could have started a new CLO role by announcing a new L&D strategy in the first few weeks, it would have been Karie Willyerd. A bestselling author and renowned thought leader in the field, with a resume packed with successful L&D leadership stints at SAP-Success Factors, Sun Microsystems, and entrepreneurial ventures, Willyerd certainly knows her stuff. Yet there was no grand vision or major strategic shift in June 2018 when she took the L&D reins at VISA. Mostly she met lots of people and listened. Over the first six months, she held meetings with more than 150 leaders at VISA as well as conducting coffee chat sessions with more than 750 employees. This was proactively building partnerships at its best. Based on these meetings and the strong ties she continued to build throughout the organization, a new L&D approach emerged that was well accepted and actively supported by VISA leaders.

Kimo Kippen, former L&D leader for Hilton, Marriott International and 2015 CLO of the year, sees these encounters to build business relationships as a way to integrate into the critical organization workstreams. He intentionally reached out to the corporate program management office leaders to learn about upcoming business initiatives and help them link the work to necessary L&D offers for success. Further, he points to initiating and regularly spending time with the CFO, IT, compliance, sustainability, and other mission-critical functions to understand their world, their leadership agenda, and their concerns.

Like winning a successful *Shark Tank* presentation, these CLO leaders value first understanding the world and concerns of their potential L&D investors so they could later craft relevant and credible solutions. I recall in my early days as talent leader for General Mills the curious reaction I was getting from my HR and L&D colleagues by setting up meetings with a wide range of business and function leaders. My ongoing check-ins with investor relations and business development leaders was regarded as unusual. Yet over time I found those two leaders in particular taught me the most about the pressures my senior leaders felt from Wall Street analysts and how the overarching business strategy evolved. Those insights provided a priceless road map to creating a business-grounded L&D agenda that the organization leaders embraced.

But the onboarding months aren't the only window to build partnerships. Nick Van Dam, former McKinsey & Company partner and CLO, launched a refreshed L&D strategy after investing months of investigation and dialogue with organization leaders throughout the consulting firm. While he certainly had a good sense of what was needed, Van Dam believed it was critical to reach out to a diverse set of partners to connect with their current thinking, recent experiences, and where they were headed. From that effort, a redirected and streamlined development strategy emerged, producing a renewed sense of commitment from McKinsey partners that the new L&D approach was relevant and critical to achieve their goals.

David Vance, former president of Caterpillar University and 2006 CLO of the year, observes that some L&D folks shy away from proactively setting time on business leader calendars and having in-depth conversations about learning from a business point of view. It's outside the comfort zone of hanging with friendly training types and the security of peer level conversations; many struggle to imagine sitting across from a senior executive. Yet if you are seeking commitment from senior management, your job is to forge ongoing working relationships with that group. In his role, Vance would touch base with the key 34 leaders of his organization at least twice a year, including the CEO, C-suite executives, and business unit leaders. He made it a priority and regular routine paralleling the business planning cycles.

Take Action

» Do a calendar audit of your time for the past 30 days. Identify any time with business leaders about their interests and plans (not selling L&D). Proactively list three to five key stakeholders you could add to your calendar for the next 30 to 90 days.

» What are two proactive steps you can take to get upstream on business initiatives or strengthen integration of L&D into organization workstreams?

» Complete the Business Partner Planner Worksheet (Job Aid 5-1).

Principle 2: Develop a Business-First Mindset and Skill Set

Recall the series of commercials the online booking site Hotels.com ran with a character called "Captain Obvious." The clueless captain would insert himself in various situations and state what was readily apparent, such as "The best way to enjoy the hotel view is to look at it." I'm sure the captain would point out that principle two is quite obvious: getting L&D support means L&D leaders need a business-first mindset.

I often wonder, why are we still talking about being a business-relevant L&D leader? Certainly nowadays the L&D field can talk the talk of business relevance more than ever before. But something is getting lost in translation. Perhaps it's not the external words but the internal mindset that is a barrier. Perhaps some like to consider themselves L&D artists. And like a lonely artist, we toil away at our craft, waiting for the world to discover us. We don't see connecting with the audience as our prime concern, but rather a frustrating and puzzling part of organization life. The reality is that management support won't come looking for you. You need to find it. That requires dropping the L&D unappreciated artist mindset and developing a new set of skills and routines.

These new skills and routines were on the flip charts of a breakout session I recently conducted. A conference organizer had called me on my challenge that most L&D conference attendees would rather join a session on the latest and coolest L&D innovation and skip a session about driving better business results. Soon I found myself in a conference room facilitating the driving business session. I was wrong at the start as the breakout room was packed and we had to offer the session twice during the conference. The session began by filling a flip chart with our favorite L&D words and abilities. On another flip chart we listed the words our business partners and senior leaders like using and the underlying abilities required. Captain Obvious would observe that those two flip charts looked very different! Then we considered the shift required to avoid our L&D-speak and increase our abilities to discuss and contribute to things like "revenue growth," "return on equity," and "profitable customer retention."

Recognizing that L&D leaders are expected to know their profession well, we explored what it would take to master business language and skills. A number of my CLO interviewees lamented that the L&D profession is still populated with some folks who are unskilled at reading income statements, balance sheets, and key business metrics. And some really lack the interest to keep up on the business side of things. They would rather be the learning artist.

As a sign of the importance of the business mindset and skills today, it was observed that it's not uncommon to see someone who had a career limited to L&D replaced by an operating leader to run a more relevant L&D department. It was noted that a sign of things gone wrong is if you overhear from other business leaders, "That new CLO really knows his stuff, but just doesn't get us." "Getting us" means getting the business, being able to easily speak the business language, and having the business skills beyond the L&D artistry.

How To

"You earn the right to advance" is one of Kimo Kippen's favorite recommendations for learning leaders. It starts with speaking in business terms and not learning-speak. Further, it means you have to connect well with a range of business folks—from the front-line operator to the HQ executives—on their terms. Knowing the language starts with having a firm grasp on the business and finance: how it makes money and what its key business drivers and metrics are. Mastering it well separates the influential, business-savvy talent development leader from the superficial, less-credible L&D artist who doesn't understand the business.

Also, learning leaders should avoid chasing the trendy new learning solution that doesn't matter that much to the business. Kippen regrets falling in love with a cutting-edge learning platform as a great solution for a problem his business didn't have. It had no business relevance or support, so it was quickly dismissed. His lesson learned was to start with the business need or objective and then find the learning solution that fits best—even if it's something simple or industry standard. Knowing the business well helps determine the best fit for learning solutions rather than bringing back something from an L&D trade show that's the latest rage.

A clever combination of the first principle on business relationship building and the second principle on business mindset and skill set comes from Ed Betof, Conference Board leader, talent development author, and former CLO for BD (Becton, Dickinson). He partnered early in his tenure with the CFO and helped deliver needed training for the finance function. It enabled him to recruit an advocate for learning from what is typically a skeptical audience and at the same time pick up on company-specific financial language and business trends. He observed that finance has much to say about budgets, business planning, and organization health. Over time, that department served as both supporter and educator for Betof and his work.

One sign of your business-first mindset is what you hold yourself accountable to deliver. Nigel Paine, former head of people development at the BBC and now prolific author and world-class consultant, finds that too many talent development managers see their role as producers of a learning process and avoid taking accountability for business impact. Other top learning leaders would agree that you need to go beyond managing a smooth-running training shop and see yourself as a partner in delivering a business goal such as reaching a new revenue target or productivity metric. Demonstrating your desire and drive to take accountability does come with a challenge. Paine recalls a debate with the senior BBC team about his proposed new learning initiative. After a while the CEO stopped the discussion and declared, "Look, let's assume Nigel knows his stuff and give him the funding to do what we hired him to do. If he fails to deliver impact, we'll fire him!" Paine was pleased to take up that accountability challenge as any other functional leader at the BBC was expected to do. Fortunately for his job, he did deliver—and support grew for even larger high-impact L&D programs over time.

Take Action

» Audit your presentations and elevator speeches about L&D to prune learning-speak and replace it with your organization's relevant business-speak.

» Consider where your accountabilities and metrics should broaden to incorporate non-L&D and HR metrics into more "line of sight" business metrics.

» Invest in refreshing or building stronger financial and business acumen by taking a finance or business strategy course. Seek out a business mentor or spend time shadowing operating leaders to learn more about their world and language.

» Reset your reading routines by regularly reviewing your business and trade industry publications and blogs. Find out what your senior leaders read and what thought leaders they follow to elevate your learning beyond L&D. (I found reading Wall Street analyst reports about my company highly informative, and it provided great opening material for conversations with my senior leaders.)

Principle 3: Be a Performance Consultant, Not an Order Taker

"Don't be the learning waitress!" These are five simple words of advice from Tamar Elkeles, this book's editor, former learning leader at Qualcomm and 2010 CLO of the Year. Elkeles has seen too many L&D practitioners happy to fall into the order-taker role, accepting what business leaders tell them to do. As with a waiter or waitress, they just simply take down the order and bring back what was requested. Worse yet, playing the L&D waiter part signals you are a reactive part of the enterprise needing to be told what to do. This trap is often rooted in a service-oriented mentality of the profession where well-intentioned L&D leaders see their role as servant leaders aiming to please. The problem with L&D waiters and order takers is that when budgets get tight, L&D is first on the menu to be cut!

My favorite question early in exploring a development opportunity is to ask the senior leader or sponsor, "If we were to implement this L&D project and achieve wild success, what business metric would move?" In other words, I like asking upfront what connects the L&D project to business priorities. Kimo Kippen would ask a similar question about what the business challenge or need is and how the leader would know if solution was successful. An encouraging response covers how building specific workforce capabilities would address a gap to achieve a business strategy or need.

The approach needed is to apply the rigor of business case development to learning programs, like any other function or business unit would use to justify investment in them. Elkeles built Qualcomm's award-winning L&D team around a similar performance consulting approach where fully understanding the need and rationale came before considering any training. And even if the L&D solution made sense, her team considered if the idea was a high enough priority and urgent enough to deal with it now.

A good rule of thumb for running learning departments is that waiting to be told what to do isn't leadership, and neither is independently conjuring up an L&D solution and then magically wishing for management sponsorship. It's better to start with meaningful business conversations, leveraged from the foundational relationships built with principle one and using the business mindset and savvy from principle two. This will uncover what is most important to the business and most aligned with senior management thinking, not what's important to L&D and aligned to the L&D agenda. Sometimes that is pushing back and saying no to a low-impact request or even a legacy program.

It takes courage and disciplined focus to lead L&D this way. I'm reminded of the newly appointed CLO of a large global technology and entertainment company who declared that if the L&D programs offered that year didn't directly fit and highly influence the five strategic priorities of the business, they would be dropped. She then followed through and ruthlessly cut legacy programs and deflected attractive L&D ideas that didn't fit her mandate. What was lost in narrowing the offerings became a respected strength of the newly focused L&D approach as business leaders took note of the enhanced contribution to what mattered most.

How To

David Vance recommends reframing the complaint of lacking management support for L&D. "What people are really saying is, 'I have an L&D agenda that the business needs to support,'" he says. "Flip that around and set in place a routine where you first discover the business strategies and gaps, then through a disciplined planning process produce L&D products that deliver to the business."

One of my favorite strategy tools is to set L&D goals that articulate the "product of the product" by adding "so that . . ." to every L&D program and initiative. It's a great discipline to clearly identify the outcome of the learning program and the product it delivers to the business. Say the L&D objective is to develop a new product training series in the second quarter. The "so that" might be that the region sales force can gain 15 percent market share this year with the new product introductions. When we lack this grounding in business importance and accountability, we over-emphasize learner engagement and satisfaction at the expense of effectively delivering or contributing to business outcomes. Of course, learners liking the experience is important, but it's really a balance of effectiveness (delivering value), efficiency (doing it productively), and engagement (learner satisfaction).

Tamar Elkeles used a proactive internal consulting model to align the work of L&D to the business priorities. On a regular basis, she would solicit the current business objectives (fast changing in a high-tech marketplace), confirm the top five priorities, and then map the skills and behaviors of the workforce necessary to achieve the priorities. From that, she employed a disciplined performance consulting approach to determine if learning should be part of the solution. She found a quarterly rhythm most effective at aligning and adjusting to keep up with the pace of business, where a balance of planning and agility was required.

Gerry Hudson-Martin, learning consultant and former CLO for Marriott International, focused on a particular business pain point as he was aligning L&D to the business. "We were getting bad press internally on the poor execution of our business projects. Our analysis showed a lack of project management competence at the heart of the problem, and we went about addressing this skills gap in the workforce," he said. "Over time, the project execution improved significantly, and the learning events provided a forum for rapid best-practice sharing and cross-fertilization of innovations . . . things that the business leaders really cared about." Hudson-Martin reflects that early in his career he might have worried about proving his L&D expertise, but over time found that worrying about what executives had on their plate mattered more. It's a simple but powerful question to keep asking yourself: What is on the plate of my senior leaders now that they worry about that I can help solve?

Adam Stedham, CEO of GP Strategies (a global learning and performance improvement company), links back to Kimo Kippen's suggestion about getting into the workstream of business areas for L&D alignment. Stedham is a proponent of hardwiring the learning requirement into the project's planning and review process. Doing so can allow the learning leader to note when the business leader misses a workforce capability component during planning and budgeting a new business initiative. Of course, it takes proactive advocacy for that change, and Kippen's strategy of building working relationships with the CFO and project management office is an example of how to position learning upstream.

Take Action

> » Consider where are your opportunities to more proactively engage in meaningful business conversations and create offerings aligned to those business strategies and needs. How can you create a regular routine to engage, align, and update key business leaders?

» Create a business-first engagement process for new L&D requests. Take a performance consulting mindset and ask for requirements to clearly define the business problem or gap, the value of providing a solution, and the appropriateness of an L&D initiative versus other alternatives.

» Require the L&D program goals to include a "so-that" statement to link the learning product to the business outcome needed. It's a test of business alignment and opportunity to weed out L&D offerings that don't provide a credible and compelling so-that linkage.

» Complete the Value-Added Analysis Worksheet (Job Aid 5-2).

Principle 4: Share to Gain Commitment

To elevate the commitment level of senior leaders to L&D initiatives, learning leaders should consider three compelling strategies. Each requires giving something up, so I've called them share-to-gain strategies, and they center around three questions: "Who makes the decisions?" "Who design and instructs?" and "Who provides the content?" As a sign of how impactful these strategies can be, during my interviews with the accomplished CLOs and L&D thought-leaders, it was remarkable how many would pause mid-sentence and then explain, "I wish I would have started that earlier!" Use these strategies to ensure stakeholder commitment.

A Decision-Making Governance Council

A self-professed numbers guy, David Vance certainly brought a strong business perspective as well as exceptional analytical and forecasting savvy when he became the president of Caterpillar University. Yet after his first year consolidating a decentralized learning community, decreasing costs, and producing high-impact programs, he realized something was missing in connecting his efforts to the overall business strategy. So in his second year he formed a learning governance council, consisting of business leaders representing the 30 divisions. The council was chartered to advise, guide, and support the enterprise L&D strategy. Vance said, "It provided great support for our programs and created advocates for L&D priorities, even when budgets were tight."

Nigel Paine went a step further when chartering his BBC learning council. "I gave these business leaders full authority to decide the L&D priorities and training budget." Of course, Paine as CLO contributed his thoughts and proposals, but it was the learning business council leaders who held the final authority. As time went on, the council would review progress and shift priorities to better match the current organizational needs.

I'm impressed with the self-confidence of these and other CLOs to share their decision-making authority. What they're giving up is the power of the traditional L&D

practitioner role in setting a strategy and budget and then trying to sell it (and defend it) to senior management. And to be clear, these advisory groups or councils weren't solely populated with other HR or L&D managers, they featured line-business leaders actively involved in making decisions with the L&D leader. While not abandoning their strategic leadership and L&D expertise role, these learning leaders gained a rock-solid alignment upfront with this decision-making body and real support of the L&D plan over time.

A Faculty Within

"I can't believe there are still CLOs not using their business leaders as teachers in this day and age. It's the most powerful commitment strategy I have seen." I could sense both astonishment and frustration as I talked to Kevin Oakes about L&D leaders struggling to secure management commitment. Oakes, CEO of the Institute for Corporate Productivity (i4cp), has seen it all in his many years in the profession, as founder of two ground-breaking learning platforms (one with Microsoft co-founder Paul Allen), ATD board chairperson, and board member of multiple learning providers. It's commonplace for L&D staff to shoulder the responsibility for learning design and delivery, augmented by external resources and faculty. So it speaks volumes that his fundamental advice to L&D leaders is to go inside, sharing the design and delivery role with line leaders.

I've had the good fortune throughout my career to have line leaders actively contributing and teaching in L&D programs, from CEOs sharing leadership challenge stories to department heads facilitating real business cases. I would add that in the short term, it's much harder to run L&D with an internal faculty. You have to figure out what role best suits their skills and interests. Their schedule can change at a moment's notice, leaving you to scramble for a replacement. And they always come with an opinion. (Hired faculty rarely cause such headaches.) However, the long-term gains of real involvement and commitment far outweigh the costs, so in the end I completely agree with Kevin Oakes. Why aren't you using your leaders in your L&D efforts?

Peer to Peer

A contemporary extension of the "faculty within" thinking is CLOs enabling more peer-to-peer knowledge sharing as a formal learning strategy. It's another "share to gain" shift as the L&D role is not to define the content and delivery choices, but rather to set up the process and system to make peer-to-peer learning simple and pervasive. Of course, informal peer sharing has been a part of the work environment for a long time, but advances in technology have expanded the reach and ease of sharing. Many would say the modern workforce is both accepting and expecting peer-to-peer knowledge sharing to do their job and grow. To some degree, the L&D role is to set it up and then get out of the way. Interestingly, line managers are quite positive about these initiatives, citing increased collaboration, employee engagement, expanded innovation, and sharing of ideas across organizational boundaries.

Consider Brain Candy, the whimsical name for HP's version of an innovative peer knowledge sharing platform. Mike Jordan, global head of talent and learning explains, "It was a response to employee focus groups, interviews and surveys about what employees wanted—rich, relevant content shared and endorsed by fellow employees worldwide." What has evolved since launch is a popular, go-to option for employees at all levels to learn, contribute, and connect with one another. As these new knowledge sharing platforms proliferate, numerous organizations are replacing static training programs with more natural and just-in-time, relevant peer learning. One such platform I've seen replaced a multi-week new employee training program packed with "you might need to know this someday" with a more popular and productive peer sharing support system that all employees now use.

How To

All three of these approaches produce high levels of management commitment and higher levels of employee satisfaction. But there are two caveats. First, "share to gain" requires L&D leaders to redefine their traditional role of domain expertise and control with a learning facilitator role. Second, it requires high levels of collaboration and confidence—collaboration with line leaders and employees alike to co-own learning and confidence that the new L&D role will be seen as impactful and valued as it was before.

Furthermore, while I'm a fan of this approach, I would strongly advise L&D leaders to apply the most appropriate innovation with the best fit for your organization. Many of my interviewees remarked that while one strategy was a great hit with the organization, they wouldn't attempt another because of organizational culture fit or maturity. The advice is to start with a firm grasp of the context and readiness for change—the culture, organization maturity, risk tolerance, management and workforce values, commitment level needed, and your own leadership capabilities—as you move forward with any of these "share to gain" strategies.

Note that all the principles in this chapter work in concert with each other. Your business relationship building approach, your business-first mindset and skill set, and business-learning connections will all be important assets as you apply the "share to gain" approach.

Take Action

» Where can you engage line leaders in the decision processes of L&D? Is a learning council a strategy you can employ to advise, align L&D priorities, and share the decision making?

» Where can you replace traditional knowledge dissemination approaches with peer sharing programs and platforms?

» Where can you increase involvement of leaders in L&D design and teaching? (See Job Aid 5-3.)

Think Like a Shark and Act Like One Too

Imagine sitting in the executive suite board room. You aren't standing or presenting; rather you have settled into your chair as a member of the top management team. You aren't an L&D leader, you are just like every other smart, hard-working executive around the table. You have a lot on your mind and hope the meeting ends early so you can get back to work. As the agenda unfolds, you watch as people join the session for a short period of time, pitch their idea, respond to questions, and then are dismissed.

In short, you are now a shark looking for a good meal.

So far you notice different styles and confidence levels of the presenters. Some do better than others. Some ideas seem of interest and others mostly irrelevant or confusing. Then the next presenter confidently strolls in and something clicks with you and the others around the table. It is someone you know because she has spent time with you before, understanding your part of the business, your strategies, your concerns. She's helped you find solutions to your challenges before. She has a well-earned reputation for execution and results. If you didn't know her at all and just listened to her proposal and Q&A, you'd think she was in finance, operations, or at least someone who knows the business well and has a passion for it. It may be surprising to some that the presenter is the company's L&D leader.

And she's a shark too.

Earlier I observed that in *Shark Tank*, the potential investors are sizing up the business value of the entrepreneur's idea. They are also evaluating the entrepreneur. Is this someone with enough business savvy to get things done? Is this someone who gets the challenges to growth? Is this someone they can trust as an equal partner with their money? If so, they're in.

The CLOs and learning leaders I interviewed about gaining management commitment all mentioned an interesting shift in their perspective as they dealt with senior management. CLOs would certainly show respect for senior management in their encounters but over time would learn to carry themselves as peers. Equal in business orientation, equal in confidence in their value-added expertise, and equal in temperament for the give-and-take nature of discussions.

The shark-like attitude and executive presence shows itself in many ways. In the L&D strategy formation stage, assertive learning leaders push back on requests to get clear on the actual problem to be solved and the business-valued indicators of success. They have the courage to say no and eliminate low-business-value learning programs. They confidently propose their learning solutions and equally request adequate resources and specific support from the business partner. If an agreement is reached on what L&D would deliver based on assumptions the business leaders made and then things changed, the learning leader goes back to reach a new agreement, with a range of flexible options.

It's 50–50 in a shark-to-shark deal.

It's the confidence to call out the risks of the L&D proposal—what could go wrong and how you will address or mitigate the downside. People mistakenly believe you should avoid talking about risk when proposing something new. I've come to appreciate that business executives are wired to ferret out risk as a primary instinct as a way to sort out the many ideas chasing few resources. Unsure people avoid or hide the risk and that makes executives nervous. Confident leaders show they've done their homework well and equally address the upside and downside of their thinking. Former CLO for PwC and 2014 CLO of the Year Tom Evans, recalls dealing with the firm partners in meetings. "I approached talent development as a business strategy enabler and execution enhancer. What was always on the mind of the executives is profitability, quality, and avoiding risk."

This mindset shows itself when things go right or wrong. They take on accountability for meaningful results, just like any other business function. They just don't manage the process, they are accountable for contributing to achieving business metrics. In the end, their partnership helps line leaders view a skilled and motivated workforce is part of their game plan to succeed.

And the L&D leader is there to help them—and the organization—win.

Job Aid 5-1: Business Partner Planner

Steps:

1. Identify six to eight business partners and key stakeholders in your organization relevant to build commitment, and complete the business partner planner worksheet. Consider getting input or sharing your plan with your manager or mentor to improve its quality and execution.
2. Look at your calendar for the past 30 days or more to note meaningful contact time with each person. Identify where you need to strengthen the relationships with these partners and capture at least two ways you can invest in building stronger contact time in the future (30 days or more).
3. Return to this worksheet at least quarterly to update your progress and revise your list. Be sure to keep track of what you learn from each encounter, such as business objectives, key metrics, and concerns.

Business Partner or Stakeholder	Role or Title	Quality of Current Relationship and Degree of Stakeholder Support for L&D (weak, average, strong)	Ideas to Strengthen Relationship	Calendar Audit: Amount of Contact Time in Past 30 Days and Next 30-Day Plan

Job Aid 5-2: Value-Add Analysis

Use this exercise periodically for your annual planning process as well as any mid-year reviews and updates.

Steps:

1. At the top of the value-add analysis worksheet, write down the top five to seven business strategies and priorities (not your L&D or HR objectives).
2. In the left column, "Current L&D Program or Offering," list all your L&D activities in descending order (greatest to least) of resource intensity (such as costs, participant time, staff required, and other resources needed to support each item).
3. In the middle column, rate each L&D program's value to the business using the following index:
    1 — **Mission Critical Contributor:** business strategy or objective cannot be accomplished without this L&D program.
    2 — **Strong Contributor:** L&D program provides a meaningful contribution to the business strategy or objective.
    3 — **Standard Contributor:** Some credible link between the L&D program and business strategy, objective, or foundational capabilities.
    4 — **Mild Contributor:** Weak line to direct business value contribution.
4. For validation and a reality check, ask a few business partners and trusted advisors to provide their own business-relevant ratings for each L&D item. Consider follow-up discussions and reflection to adjust any score differences.
5. In the right column, write down ways to strengthen investment and execution of type 1 and 2 contributors and ways to reduce or eliminate 3 and 4 contributors.

Use the bottom part of the worksheet to identify potential L&D type 1 and 2 contributors for business strategies and objectives not yet addressed by current offerings.

Top Business Strategies and Priorities		
Current L&D Program or Offering	Business Relevance Index	Actions to Consider
New L&D programs to add with high business relevance		

Job Aid 5-3: Strategies for Leaders as Teachers

Top Roles for Leaders in Instructing	Useful Methods of Learning Involving Leader-Teachers	Preparing Leaders for Their Role
• Speaking or storytelling about personal experiences • Teaching, co-teaching, or facilitating a workshop • Teaching a single class or module • Participating in new-hire onboarding • Guiding and mentoring experiential learning	• Instructor-led live classes • Other live learning events (e.g., network meetings and discussion groups) • Webinars • Digital learning modules, MOOCs, and podcasts • Simulations and gamification • Organization social media contribution	• Involvement in content selection and design • Clarify roles and expectations in learning • Help determine workforce learning needs and solutions • Debrief after sessions for feedback and improvement • Provide train-the-trainer support after assessing abilities • Partner new leader-teachers with learning professionals

Adapted from ATD (2015).

6

The Talent Behind an Award-Winning Learning Team

Gale Halsey

It's all about the people. Great learning leaders build great learning teams. Developing, transforming, and supporting a learning team enables the learning function to be a strategic asset to any organization.

A leader is rarely given the opportunity to build a team from scratch, whether they are the new head of a learning organization or one who has been tasked to transform it. More often, a leader has been given a team of people with various capabilities, backgrounds, and mindsets. They are also likely to face one of two business challenges: Grow the team's capabilities quickly to match rapid organizational growth, or shrink the team and budget while delivering more content, more quickly, and for less money than the year before. Both of these conditions—growth and decline—present opportunities to build strategic learning teams that meet organizational challenges with speed, quality, and cost effectiveness.

Traditional learning design methods like ADDIE (analysis, design, development, implementation, and evaluation) are quickly becoming insufficient for businesses in states of growth or decline. While the principles remain relevant, the application, the design methods, and the technologies are quickly changing. Teams must quickly and continuously improve skills, acumen, and technical literacy as well as competencies in multiple areas like human-centered design and Agile development.

The hardest change of all is mindset: The mindset that all learning should come from internal L&D professionals alone stifles innovation. This is perhaps the hardest part of a learning transformation—change can be threatening, and many organizations don't spend the time required to invest and engage in continuously challenging paradigms and developing learning professionals.

In this chapter, I'll offer tips for putting together a team capable of making your learning organization strategic. I start with how building that team actually begins first with an assessment of the business. Rather than assess your team's knowledge and skills against unaligned learning and development goals, you need to fully understand what the business needs. Whether you have a business operations background or a talent development one, you can leverage your previous experience to grow your acumen in the other.

Next, I show how you can use awards criteria to determine what learning and development skills you need to fill gaps in your team to deliver true business value. In fact, the three most needed learning skills match those in demand by business teams: understanding the customer, practicing Agile learning development, and continuously embracing everyday technologies. As a learning leader, you have many opportunities to either build or buy these skills to round out your staff. The key is determining the right one for the right solution.

In all, the team is the gateway to a truly strategic learning organization.

Assess Business Needs First

The most successful learning leaders first collect data on business requirements, assess their own ability to deliver these requirements, and only then evaluate their team. It is essential to understand which experiences, capabilities, and relationships are required for success in this position.

"When you take on a new position, it is critical to resist the urge to jump in and start working," says Dawn Rowley, co-founder of BenchStrength Coaching. "Purposeful data gathering is needed to make sure you understand the business strategies and the capabilities that are required to deliver them. It is also important to ask business leaders about their perspective on your team: What is the reputation of your organization; are there any unfilled expectations?"

To gather information on the business, here are some direct questions to ask:
» What is the overall business strategy?
» What are the capabilities required to deliver that strategy in the now, near, and far?
» What are the talent gaps in the organization?
» Which capabilities should my organization build, buy, or borrow?
» Are there analytics that would be helpful?
» What are the expectations of myself and my team?
» Whom will I need to influence and which team members can help me?
» How can I build relationships within my team and within my organization, and, equally as important, which relationships will I need to cultivate outside my organization to help me deliver strategic products and services?
» What are your priorities in the now, near, and far?

"Great leaders continue to ask questions," continues Rowley. "Solicit input from business leaders frequently—not just at the start of an assignment."

You can bring these questions to your organization's key stakeholders such as the CEO, CHRO, CFO, and business unit leaders. But you should also target others, especially those who influence the C-suite. Identifying these influencers and up-and-coming key talent and building those relationships can turn them into formal ambassadors or informal advocates for your work. In addition, you should forecast which stakeholders might be grading your organization in six months, one year, and even five years and determine what they value to maintain strong future alignment and stakeholder buy-in.

Clearly prioritizing business objectives and understanding expectations will give you a compass with which to assess yourself and your team. Your team can be crushed under the weight of trying to be all things to all people. Even learning teams with near unlimited budgets—although rare—must identify short-term wins. Following your company's business planning process is important to ensure that ongoing content maintenance, technology, and development needs are included in forward-planning. The key for being strategic is to pick three priorities based on the inputs from your customers and align them against your executive stakeholders' input.

Do You Have the Necessary Skills?

For many years, organizations have held varied, conflicting views about whether a business person or a learning professional should lead the learning organization. The debate is especially pronounced in organizations that build technical or functional learning solutions. This debate often stems from perceptions of the required learning curve and past value-add of the learning organization to the business.

One viewpoint: "All learning leaders must deeply understand the business and so should their teams. I believe that you can teach learning professionals the business faster than you can teach business professionals about learning."

Here are a few tips for building your team's business acumen quickly:

» Read industry publications and blogs.
» Scan internal websites.
» Shadow leaders in key meetings and on key days.
» Call CLOs or their counterparts in similar industries.
» Visit customers.
» Attend business conferences, not just "learning" conferences.

A contrary viewpoint: "I'm a business professional leading learning professionals. Of course I must appreciate the science of learning, but I can attend business meetings and help anticipate, communicate, and quickly make changes. I find my business background helpful when influencing other business leaders. In my structure, my top leaders are business professionals, and they lead instructional system designers. I rely upon and value the feedback from ISD and, at times, push back to ensure we deliver a quality product."

Here are a few tips for building your team's learning capability quickly:

» Phone a friend: Call other CLOs and develop your network. If you need connections, reach out to ATD or other professional organizations for contacts.

» Attend conferences and network with colleagues.

» Share your team: Pair up with other companies' learning professionals and create your own conference or learning day. Share techniques and strategies for developing content.

In the end, both approaches work. Successful learning leaders supplement their own capability gaps and help their teams align to the business.

What Makes for an Award-Winning Team?

Before you complete the initial assessments of the business, yourself, and your team, you must understand what defines award-winning from an external perspective.

Research and interview organizations like ATD, i4CP, and SHRM to find out about emerging practices. If you want to build an award-winning team, you must know the criteria for the awards. One of the biggest mistakes a new or existing learning leader can make is to become too insular, focus too inwardly on delivery based on current tech and capabilities, and assume applying for awards is a waste of time because of politics, time, or money. In reality, awards are about learning as much as recognition. Inherent in award criteria are nuggets about learning excellence for which leaders and their teams should become intimately familiar. The various award criteria are also a basis for self- and team-assessment.

"When I first took over as CLO, I thought that awards were just about branding my organization. I felt it was all a political game," says Rob Lauber, CLO of McDonalds. "However, as I attended more conferences and analyzed the award criteria, I realized that these were a source of truth for me: Am I paying attention to the right KPIs? Do I have the skills in my team to be able to deliver or do I need to build them? Are there alternative ways to deliver and develop content that are faster, cheaper, and better than what we can deliver today? What do the awards have in common and why? What is changing every year?"

Once you've considered best practices and what excellence looks like, it is time to reassess with these questions:

» What did you learn from others? How was the bar raised and how do teams respond?

» How are you stacking up as a leader?

» What's changing in customer and industry practices?

» Are your team's processes modern? Are there ways to adopt new Agile practices?

» What new technologies could make your team more effective and efficient?

» How do you help your team learn about award-winning practices and apply them to everyday business?

Match Learning Capabilities With Business Capabilities

Perhaps shockingly, and yet fortunately for learning leaders, the biggest capability gaps in learning professionals are also the gaps facing many businesses. They include understanding the customer (human-centered design), adopting Agile and an Agile mindset and learning design, and using big technology platforms and solutions as well as smaller technologies in the right way and at the right time.

Human-Centered Design

As the art, science, and technology of learning continues to evolve, so do your customers' expectations. How do you ensure your team truly understands the needs of its customers? Much like business product and service design can benefit from placing customer needs front and center, learning leaders and professionals need to master techniques and tools from human-centered design. Consider this CLO's tale of how her team failed to understand their customers' true needs and ended up backing a solution based more on flash than substance.

A CLO at a Fortune 10 company once shared her biggest mistake with a crowd of hundreds: She cost her company millions of dollars because she truly didn't understand how her customer consumed learning. She listened to other companies and vendors talk about their sleek learning portals—award-winning learning management systems that included fun, five-star rating feedback capability and splashy landing sites. As all good CLOs would do, she asked her team to be customer-centered and conduct numerous focus groups on the employee experience, gathering global input on content and appearance before implementing this new shiny global system. The global project team worked countless hours to standardize processes and policies. Initially the team received glowing feedback, but usage wasn't improving after the initial uptick from the employee launch. She was convinced that this was just a communication or marketing issue, and that she just needed to get the word out in a more meaningful way. Again, her team assembled focus groups and engaged marketing experts to understand how to market this new system in a better, employee-friendly way. Again, the usage initially ticked up, and then tapered.

This CLO did a quick experiment: She sat with different employees and asked them to show her how they found learning content. Her company had an intranet site with a search function. In all cases, they typed in the search function—just like they did with their search engine at home—and came up with thousands of entries not relevant to their search, causing hours of frustration or simply loss of interest. Some were tenacious enough to ask their supervisor. When she watched their supervisors look for the learning content, they did the same thing—even though the intranet site had a key link on the home page to the content. When she asked employees to show her what they did after a class or online viewing, employees told her they were not interested in filling out the five-star rating. Why? Most classes were mandatory or dictated by the job so they wouldn't use a star rating to choose a class. "I'm not buying a product—I have to take the class," they told her.

Instead of implementing a shiny LMS, money would have been better spent up-front linking and cleaning the corporate search engine. Following human-centered design practices might've helped her avoid adopting an expensive solution or at least making the expensive solution more effective. Perhaps she still needed the LMS, but it would have been more effective with a better lens on the customers' pain points. This is one example of why learning teams must build capability around customer-centered design processes.

To prevent making similar mistakes here's a human-centered design tip: Observe what, how, and when people learn things on their own. What triggers them to find a learning resource? How do they find it? What channels do they use and why? There are human centered design tools that help you map a customer's experience and pain points, thus uncovering the root cause of a performance problem. Search for human-centered design tools and training online or ask a consultant.

Agile Learning and Development

Most learning leaders realize that traditional content development cycles are too slow to keep up with organizations' needs, but struggle to understand how to pivot from traditional approaches. The more traditional approach is ADDIE, which is a lengthy five-step process. This linear approach works well if you have content with a long shelf life and customers can wait for the solution. The goal of this approach is quality and completeness. Its limitations are speed and relevancy. In contrast, Agile learning design involves business professionals and learning professionals co-creating content, iterating, testing as the content is designed, and continually prioritizing changes throughout the process. Learning leaders can champion co-creation and collaboration by positioning the learning organization as an aligned business partner.

Agile content development and project management was initially derived from the technology field to create software. It is a structured process that includes concepts like frequent reiteration, daily check-in meetings with developers and business owners, lists of potential changes, frequent prioritization, and frequent release of software. The process helps cut development time and costs substantially, while improving customer satisfaction and KPIs drastically.

Consider an example. A learning leader was asked to develop learning materials associated with a new performance management process. He had six weeks to design, develop, and evaluate the content. He first tried the traditional process:

1. Assign instructional designers to work with subject matter experts to conduct a proper needs assessment and then co-develop the content.

2. Engage the global team to ensure relevancy though weekly meetings and reviews.
3. Test the materials using the HR team as pilot "learners" to evaluate the content prior to launch.

He realized after the third week that the project was severely behind. He found out that the instructional designers and SMEs were arguing about the content. One thought that the material was irrelevant for experienced supervisors, and the other thought that experienced supervisors would benefit from basic overviews and refreshers. One believed that the learning channel should consist of short videos, and the other believed that it should be in person. The in-depth needs assessment process was cut short due to the tight timeline and the dreaded phrase: "Don't worry, I know my customer."

The global contacts were not helping either. One person from each region was assigned to help and give feedback, but at least one person was always absent from the meetings, and most were not reading the content until the night prior. This caused re-work and slow-downs.

In the fifth week, the content was "finalized" with just enough time to do one session with human resources volunteers. There was not enough time to socialize with key stakeholders and sponsors, and ultimately, the content was at best ignored.

So how would you rewrite this story using an Agile approach?

The learning leader assembles a cross-functional group, which will stay together full-time as an Agile team. He finds them a space (physical or virtual) to collaborate and appoints an Agile project manager. The product sponsor is the one who will continually evaluate the content and help make decisions about additional content in the backlogs—a way to introduce and prioritize new sections of content or channels.

The team develops user profiles based on interviews and observation of customers. They use these profiles as they storyboard the content and develop prototypes to test with the users.

Based on the feedback, they can rapidly iterate. They check in the with the product owner regularly. The have daily stand-ups where they provide progress updates with the global team members in case they need to quickly make changes.

The result: There is no need to use HR as evaluators, and the product sponsor is informed throughout and can guide needs to pivot so the design meets the customers' needs.

More than ever, learning leaders are pushing their teams to apply these concepts to learning and development processes, embrace iterative design, and allow for adaptation to changes. Another approach is Rapid Content Development (RCD), used most frequently for e-learning. This approach uses templates so that content can be reused and changes can be easily adapted throughout the content shelf-life.

"When looking across the globe, RCD is critical," explains Sheila Covert-Weiss, former L&OD leader, South America, for a Fortune 15 company. "We tried using

ADDIE in the regions (South America and Mexico) but the time delay cost us the relationship and trust with the business. We used RCD methodology to quickly plug the issues and proposed solutions and apply throughout the region. Customers were engaged and saw the savings and successes. We were nimble and adaptable and very valuable to the business, a big win-win."

Agile has many variations and methods, but for learning content development they have a few main components in common:

» In ADDIE, collaborative customer brainstorming and contracting occurs upfront. In Agile, all stakeholders need to be involved in the upfront contracting, but they hold the point of view lightly because changes frequently happen based on learning along the process.
» Smaller segments of the course are discussed rather than the project as a whole.
» The use of sprints or full-time off-sites where members devote their full attention to the project helps avoid lag time from developing parts of the course "on the side of a person's desk" in conjunction with other projects. This allows teams to focus and move forward without losing momentum.
» Frequent check-ins and prioritized changes are made with key stakeholders as ideas and new information are generated.

Big and Small Technologies

A four-year-old can take videos. A 14-year-old can talk to people around the world using social media or video games. A 17-year-old can develop and edit an award-winning documentary using only a smartphone. And, every year, the age of the human and the accessibility of technologies are brought closer together. Why do we think that learning professionals shouldn't be using the same technologies as their customers to develop content?

Technology is becoming cheaper and more attainable for the general public. This means consumers—and learners—are more willing to accept less picture-perfect content than ever before. For example, polished video is becoming a thing of luxury. In fact, scripted video is becoming less accepted by end users because it is the medium they use in life outside work. Thankfully, this means that every learning professional can become a "small" technology expert—small technologies are technology tools that are accessible with minimal instruction and cost. Encouraging your trainers and learning professionals to embrace small technologies can be your biggest gift because you don't have to spend thousands of dollars for a video shoot. Other small technologies, like social media, blogging software, and mobile software, can bring impact without big budgets. "Big" technology professionals like videographers are still relevant, but you don't have to hire a videographer and set up a green room for every video. You just have to upskill your learning professionals to develop instructionally sound content cheaply and quickly using the available technologies. You may not even need a big technology solution such as an LMS if you have a company search engine and web-based or cloud-based search and storage system.

So how do you upskill? Jonathon Casterline is an instructional system designer (ISD) supporting large corporations. He was an early adopter of small technologies and was often called upon to help with projects where I work. He saw a need to upskill peers on small technology solutions—and he gave the gift of his time and experience by creating "TechieTalk" Discussion Forums, a monthly community of practice session for our ISDs and learning and development team members.

Casterline and others on the team provide tips and tricks, demonstrations, and hands-on practice sessions using video, audio, multimedia, and software development tools. "TechieTalks allow our training professionals a chance to share their experiences and familiarize themselves with the expanding technical skills that ISDs need to produce media-rich and engaging content," explains Casterline. "The sessions are a safe place for attendees to practice and learn with support from their peers. Attendees help choose the topics, and their input directs the sessions to be relevant to their needs. TechieTalks have made a direct and immediate impact on our ISDs' projects, and as a bonus, I have learned from those that attend the sessions too." Community learning forums that create shared learning are perfect channels to introduce new technologies.

Casterline says that upskilling the team costs less than sourcing professionals and cuts the cost and speed of developing learning solutions. There is still a need for big technologies but it can be easily supplemented by building capability within our ISD experts.

Making Development of the Learning Team an Emphasis

Despite the need to match learning capabilities with business capabilities, the learning team often neglects its own development. Hence, the proverb "The shoemaker's children go barefoot" is often used when describing learning for learning professionals. I usually hear a few common excuses masked as reasons for why this is so:

» Learning professionals feel selfish about taking time away to work on themselves when customers require support.
» There are too many meetings and not enough self-reflection.
» Budget formation never includes learning for the learning team.
» Self and team learning are not prioritized over learning for others.
» Learning is not embedded in meetings, forums, or ways of working.
» The learning leader sets no expectations for development.

Everything changes—every day and in every way. What are the best practices for continuing to win recognition from internal stakeholders and external sources? How does a leader leverage the collective wisdom of the team rather than engaging a few high performers? How does the leader create the daily environment to bring new ideas and learning content into the learning organization? Setting expectations of a team to continually learn and creating an environment to share and implement those lessons is at the heart of a learning organization. It should be no shock that those are the conditions that must exist within a learning team.

Governance is a stale word that implies bureaucracy and meeting fatigue. At the heart of good governance is a mechanism to include learning in every forum, meeting, and decision-making body. For example, most functions within the business hold all-employee meetings. Best-in-class learning organizations can include a learning component in their meetings, such as time for reflection, dialogue, and skill development.

"We found a series of four small book parables and questions to spark dialogue relevant to our team," says Sheila Covert-Weiss. "We created four teams across the organization and asked them to present one book at each all-employee meeting. We told each team they could present in a format of their choice, with the most creative team winning the honor of being recognized. The formats ranged from puppet shows to skits to music productions. It was an amazing team-building exercise as well as a fun way to create learning and dialogue."

In addition, internal communities of practice, much like TechieTalks, are still a tried-and-true format for upskilling teams.

"Our global community of practice was attended by almost 70 learning professionals each month," says Covert-Weiss. "We videotaped each session so that people could access the topics at any time around the world. The need for global upskilling and sharing is becoming more and more important. Each region or individual can bring best practices to the forums. External and internal guests should be presenters on critical topics."

Consultants and vendors can also be great sources of learning. Invite a partner to present at every major meeting to ensure all employees reap the knowledge from these rich sources of benchmarking data.

All of these practices—human-centered design, an Agile mindset and Agile project management, and big and small technology adoption—are straightforward. The key to success is to prioritize and continually re-evaluate learning for learning professionals.

When to Buy

There might come a time, though, when you can't always build the skills your learning team needs to meet business demands. Deciding whether you might need to leverage an external vendor depends on many factors, such as geography, cost, time to deliver, shelf-life, and capability required.

Rob Lauber tells new CLOs that they should keep a handful of internal experts but rely on external sourcing of content development by project: "This ensures you maintain your internal standards and quality checks, but enjoy the flexibility and fresh perspective from hiring external candidates," he says.

Lauber also believes that you don't need large companies to source talent. "I've enjoyed working with a smaller company who makes my company a priority. We don't need to retrain them on formats and standards, but the small size allows them to be nimble enough to accommodate changing business expectations."

He suggests that new learning leaders call other CLOs for vendor referrals. "Your CLO network will be your best source of information and mentoring."

Geography can also play a large role in determining whether to buy or build capability. Let's consider a case study of global content development gone wrong.

A CLO of a Fortune 15 company was faced with developing a global leadership program for mid-level supervisors. She thought the best way to develop the content was to create a small global team of learning professionals. She also wanted to demonstrate that content could be developed outside the world headquarters based in the United States. Her European region team volunteered to develop the content with input from learning professionals in each region.

At first, everything seemed to be going smoothly. The content development was moving forward with input from customers. The team met weekly to continue the content development. With much fanfare, the new leadership program was launched in the United Kingdom. The feedback was fantastic. Her team was given kudos for being globally minded.

As the program was being launched in other regions, however issues emerged. For starters, industry conditions worsened. Business leaders from China and South America could not afford the materials, external facilitator daily rates, or the facilitator travel required to deliver the new experience. No problem, the CLO thought. We can source local facilitators internally. However, these strategies required extensive train-the-trainer time and deep knowledge of the content—too much time and cost to use internal resources. The next obvious answer was to ask the global vendor to supply facilitators from a local vendor. Her team quickly informed her that the global vendor didn't have any local facilitators, and it would take too much time to find and train them to deliver the content. She thus faced a facilitator shortage.

The next issue lay with the content. The content was met with fanfare in Europe and the United States, but in South America and China by the local learning leaders. It needed to be adapted significantly. Other content issues ranged from lack of ISD expertise within the market and universities, to issues of language translation, culture relevancy, and general misalignment of customer needs and market maturity.

What was initially heralded as a long-awaited, award-winning experiential leadership program became a shelf item for all but the U.S. and European markets.

Here are some factors to consider when buying learning expertise:

» Don't assume ISD and instructor capability is readily available internally or externally in all markets. After this experience, the CLO asked her senior ISDs to train on-site in those regions, with ongoing follow-up and support via communities of practice.

» Leadership and technical programs will likely need a "top" hat based on cultural and employee needs. Timelines and development costs must account for this reality.

» Translation needs can be met externally, but must be reviewed in depth by learning professionals. Ensure the budget and timeline can account for these variances. Translation technology has improved drastically, but it cannot replace knowledge of local cultural nuances.

» How global is global? Learning leaders should ask vendors for local facilitators and content developers upfront in the contracting process.

» Internal capacity to develop is also a factor, especially for technical content. If the content has a short shelf life and is not proprietary, it is better to curate it. If learning professionals take a year to design content that is quickly updated, the learning team is not serving the business.

The Talent Behind the Curtain

There is no perfect script for building a strategic learning team. The art and science of learning is constantly changing, as are customers' expectations and technology advances. Success is defined by how a learning leader understands the business strategy, the people, and the methods to continually adapt.

It starts with a leader who is diligent in conducting three different types of assessment: business needs, background, and expertise of themselves and their top learning leaders, in addition to an ability to "raise their gaze" to understand the changing definition of award-winning.

The next assessment requires evaluating a team against the definition of award-winning and the top capabilities required by the team. The question of whether to build or buy (or curate) is then framed against realities such as speed to develop, team capacity, shelf life, translations, and local versus global requirements.

There will always be a need for internal learning and capability building. The best learning organizations embed learning into existing forums, create space for learning via communities of practice, and expect and support internal experts who continuously learn. They expose their teams to the best business and professional forums. And, finally, they apply for awards to learn from others and seek feedback.

As the proverbial award-show curtain closes, and the team takes a bow, it is time to reassess and get ready for the next show.

7

Leaders as Teachers

Jayne Johnson

> Organizational leaders make vital friends of the learning function. Build them, support them, and manage them. These learning ambassadors affect the learning brand and reputation.

A great deal has been written about the subject of leaders as teachers (LAT) over the years. In fact, my good friend Ed Betof, who is known in many circles as the "Father of LAT," has written several books, presented at conferences, and been at the center of many interviews on the subject. When it comes to building a strategic learning organization, getting your leaders involved in the learning that happens throughout the business is the most effective way to ensure that learning aligns to what matters most.

With close to 50 percent of the American workplace made up of Millennials and, by 2025, an estimated 75 percent of the global workforce being Millennials, gone are the days when you bring a group of people together for a week at a time to learn about leadership development by inviting a few senior leaders to "teach" the class armed with 160 PowerPoint slides for the one-hour session. Today's talent expects much more than that. They want something relevant, compelling, and readily available that they can immediately apply in their own world.

In this chapter I will review some of the benefits associated with LAT. I include not only the value to the organization, but also to the leader themselves, the learner, and the L&D function. I will then explore ideas for selecting the right leaders for LAT and preparing them. Finally, I will get into new forms or applications of LAT that are emerging in the workplace today.

Benefits to the Organization

Let's start with the organization. Why should you bother introducing a model of LAT, or for those of you who have already implemented it, why should you continue your efforts?

Every good company wants to attract, develop, and retain only the very best talent. In a recent study by Udemy, the *2018 Millennials at Work Report*, 42 percent of those surveyed said L&D was the second-most important benefit when deciding where to work, only behind healthcare (48 percent). Done well, LAT is a surefire way to cultivate a learning culture and appeal to your strongest talent. When leaders are willing to invest their precious time preparing and participating in teaching events, they become role models for the rest of the organization and reinforce that development is a priority.

The organization also benefits by having senior leaders cascade key messages and priorities of the company. When I worked at Crotonville, GE's corporate university where 10,000 leaders a year were selected to attend a prestigious cornerstone leadership program, we set expectations with the learners that they had a responsibility to continue cascading the messages and priorities they learned about while at Crotonville to their own teams. It was a very effective way to ensure alignment around the company's strategic objectives and focus people on the priorities that were critical to business success. During my many years with the company, the top leaders of GE would kick off every year in Boca Raton, Florida, to establish the strategic priorities of the company, ranging from what industries to exit or enter to evaluating new ways of doing business, like the introduction of "Boundarylessness" (GE's version of accountability and collaboration). Immediately following the Boca meeting, the Crotonville staff would work around the clock identifying the appropriate courses with which to integrate the new concepts. We would scour academia for world-class experts on the subject and identify internal leaders at GE who could share best practices and lessons learned on the topic. Learners who came to Crotonville felt a sense of pride that they were hearing the latest news directly from the CEO, including Jack Welch and Jeff Immelt during my tenure, who took the time out of their busy schedules to address the learners directly.

Crotonville become the place where GE leaders came to learn new ways of thinking, expanding their perspectives and experiencing the LAT practices so they could carry on the torch in their own GE businesses. Many business leaders felt a responsibility for sharing the messages they heard while at Crotonville and would plan debrief sessions with their own teams upon returning from class.

Benefits to the Leader

LAT also helps promote development for the leaders who are doing the teaching. Aristotle once said, "Those who know, do; those that understand, teach." Preparing is a very reflective process. Depending on the topic, the leader may need to think about and remember past experiences from their career that help reinforce a teachable moment. As Dave DeFilippo, founder of DeFilippo Leadership, and executive coach in Harvard Business School's executive education programs told me during a recent conversation on the topic, "LAT is a high-wire act. You can really look bad. You have to prepare." So when leaders practice active teaching, it promotes their own learning and improves their ability to self-reflect. And when they have a positive experience, it encourages them to want to do more of it, creating a positive and repetitive cycle.

Leaders also learn new information and gain new perspectives that they wouldn't have been exposed to normally. I've spoken to many leaders who claim they learn more during their experience than the learners. Whether a participant offers some insight about the business strategy, asks a provocative question regarding the current approach, or proposes a different perspective, these are all opportunities for leaders to open their minds and consider different viewpoints.

Another very important benefit to the leaders who teach is the opportunity to interact with a group of talent beyond their current network. Some leaders shamelessly admit to scouting talent when they participate in a workshop. What better way to meet new, talented individuals than by challenging the group with provocative questions about the business and seeing what emerges? I recall numerous times when learners would attend a leadership program at Crotonville and a few months later I would learn that they had moved to new jobs in a different part of the company. Nine times out of 10 they moved to a part of the business led by the person who was an LAT. The learners made a great impression, either by asking a powerful question, offering a new viewpoint, debating a point made by the speaker (respectfully), or starting a conversation with the leader following the presentation, which then led to further discussions about career opportunities. This way of acquiring talent reduces the uncertainty of making an external hire based on a couple of interviews. And we all know that promoting internal talent sends a powerful message to the rest of the organization and reduces the chance for making a poor choice with an external hire who may not be a strong cultural fit.

Benefits to the Learner

The learner also gains value in an organization that uses an LAT approach. The most obvious is the opportunity to learn from the experiences and perspectives of successful leaders, and role models of the organization. They come with a completely different background than the learner, different strengths, development needs, challenges, lessons learned, and successes. The stories they tell provide the learners an opportunity to see a day in the life of someone who thinks and acts differently. Rich discussion can emerge by simply talking about a business scenario and listening to how the leader responded to it. This opens the discussion up to the class to see how others might have approached the situation. I remember with fondness being in classes at Crotonville, listening to the questions or responses of my colleagues. I would always ask myself, "Now why do I think they asked that question?" and "Where are they going with that response?" It helped me to get outside my automatic reaction to try to see the situation from someone else's perspective.

As discussed, the learner has an opportunity to make a positive impression on the leader, which can result in expanded job responsibilities within the same function or business unit or even within a different part of the company. And if things don't always lead to a new job, it can also be an opportunity to enlist the help of a new mentor or simply add someone to your network who you can turn to when you'd like to bounce ideas off someone with an objective mindset.

The last benefit to the learner is often the one most unrealized. That is the benefit of learning reinforcement to aid in remembering what was learned and increasing the chances of changing behavior. I am referring to the Ebbinghaus forgetting curve. Back in 1885, Hermann Ebbinghaus, a German psychologist, studied the relative strength of memory over a short period of time. From his studies he was able to determine the amount of time it takes to forget information. He also was able to hypothesize on the effects of "overlearning" or reinforcing material. My experience is that forced reflection and teaching others what you've learned bears out Ebbinghaus' findings on memory. Whenever anyone on my team attends a conference, I always ask them to come back and share the highlights with the rest of the team. Not only are you spreading the wealth by sharing lessons learned from the conference with others, but you're forcing the learner to reflect and provide valuable insights regarding their experiences, which increases the likelihood that they will remember these lessons themselves and try one of the recommendations or alter their behavior to adopt a new skill or mindset.

Benefits to the L&D Function

And finally, let's not forget about the L&D function. After all, a lot of work goes into selecting the right leaders, preparing the leaders, and ensuring the message is aligned with the content of the workshop. There is obviously the opportunity to save dollars because you are leveraging the knowledge and wisdom of your internal talent while avoiding the need to hire consultants or other external subject matter experts.

Arguably one of the best outcomes is the strong partnership formed with the functional leaders of the business. The role of L&D is to set the leader up for a successful experience. Facilitators in your L&D team will act as coaches, review materials, help shape their stories, and connect the dots with key points along the way. In fact, L&D's role is a vital part of the equation. I can't tell you how many times I've invited leaders to speak to a class and they're caught off guard when I make an appointment with them to prepare in advance of the class. We will cover ways of preparing leaders for their role later in this chapter, but the important point here is your role as the L&D leader is to ensure that this LAT will be a valuable experience for the leader and the learners.

That means you may have to deliver some tough messages to your leader if they were planning to share 100 PowerPoint slides and simply "talk at" the audience. You may have to spend dedicated time with the leader coaching them and helping them identify their own stories that will drive a point home, or create an engaging two-way exercise where the learners have an opportunity to reflect, practice, and apply concepts being shared by the LAT.

Criteria for Selecting the Best LATs

Now that we've covered the benefits of LATs, how do you decide which leaders will make the best teachers? The process for selecting them will of course depend on a few factors, including the context of the program you are offering as well as the current company culture and whether LAT is a common practice.

Let's assume you've never implemented an LAT approach and you are looking to introduce the concept for the first time for a new leadership development program you've created for your high-potential talent. Where do you start? Getting your CEO to commit to speak at a program or record a podcast would be an ideal starting point. Of course, this assumes your CEO is inspirational and will stay on point in terms of the message you'd like them to deliver. Even if your CEO isn't known as an inspiring leader, you should still happily welcome them into your class because having the CEO participate sends a message to other senior leaders that supporting the development of talent is a priority. This makes your job of recruiting others easier in the future.

Once you've had the CEO come to one of your classes or they've participated in some other fashion, you're now looking for other leaders to join. How do you decide who to go to first? Naturally, it will depend on the topic you want the leader to speak to. For example, if you need someone who can address the strategic priorities or financial health of the company, you will likely turn to your CFO or COO. But if you are looking for someone who can speak to a more generic topic, like the importance of developing talent for the future of the organization or taking risks on talent to fill key roles within the function, then your possibilities are far greater. You can start with your program sponsor, assuming you have one. They should be able to suggest leaders in the organization who could deliver such a message in a compelling way.

If you don't have a formal sponsor for your training or development program, I would tap into your executive leadership team. Having made connections to this team, you will likely know many of their attributes yourself. Do any of them jump out to you as being a role model in the area you are covering? Do they have a track record for developing talent on their own team? Have any of them taken a chance on an "unknown" talent in the past that proved successful?

If you don't know your executive team very well because you are new to the company, this is a perfect excuse for you to schedule meetings with each of them, introduce yourself and your plans for the L&D function, and gain support for the program you are launching. As you meet with the leadership team, you should prepare questions to ask them that will help you evaluate whether they would make a good LAT themselves, or at the very least, have recommendations for you on which of their colleagues you should be meeting with.

When I was at Keurig Green Mountain, I was fortunate that my CEO understood the importance of talent development and made it a priority on his agenda. So when I launched a new leadership program targeted at our director population from across the company, I invited him to join us and he willingly accepted. I reviewed the key components of the workshop with him and encouraged him to speak about strategic thinking, one of the backbones for the workshop. Since I was new to the company at the time and I didn't have experience working with our leadership team, I asked him if he wanted me to prepare talking points or slides. His preference was to keep it more casual, and he did a fabulous job and had the participants on the edge of their chairs the entire time. During his talk he mentioned a couple other individuals on his leadership team, speaking about some of their key priorities, challenges, and successes. I then used that as an opportunity to approach the leaders he mentioned and shamelessly invited them to speak at a future class, letting them know that the CEO had mentioned their critical initiatives to the class. How could they refuse my invitation? I would then work with each of the leaders individually until I got to know their capabilities as an LAT and their personal styles.

To summarize the characteristics to consider when selecting LAT candidates, titles always help as they are a draw to your learners but also help you in recruiting other leaders for future classes. Second, you want to target role models in the organization, those who are strong performers. Self-confidence may be an obvious characteristic you look for in your LATs but also consider a willingness to show vulnerability with the class—as Brene Brown said, "Vulnerability is not weakness; it's our greatest measure of courage."

Preparing Leaders for Their Role as LAT

With a leader or squad of leaders selected, you and your team can set out to prepare them for the LAT role. This preparation is not difficult or vastly time consuming, but it does require the leader to reflect on their career. Depending on the topic they will be covering they may need to dig deep into their past experiences. Typically a leader will ask you, "So what do you want me to say?" You can explain the themes you are targeting, but the stories need to come from them. It's personal. You can suggest they think back through their careers and highlight the top three to five lessons learned (such as anecdotes from career transitions, mistakes, successes, and challenges). They may not have ever done such reflection before in a teacher capacity. But this process is powerful. Done well, not only will the LATs improve their ability to be reflective but they will be role modeling for the participants how to be reflective in the moment.

Another best practice in preparing leaders for their role is to encourage them to have a dialogue rather than a monologue. They should prepare a couple of challenging questions and compelling stories. Have them practice on you or your team. Provide feedback and be honest with them. The skilled LATs know how to engage participants in stimulating dialogue and how to take them to the edge of their own comfort zone. It's alright to take risks, letting the discussions flow freely while staying on topic.

Ideas for Deploying Your LATs

With the groundwork of selecting and preparing LATs laid, what are some modern, innovative ways to deploy them? We've all heard of the companies known for having a culture that promotes LATs, including GE, Boeing, Deloitte, and BD. The typical vision that comes to mind when we think of leaders playing the teacher role is when they come into a class and "teach" using lessons learned, experiences, or stories from their past. That style of LAT will always have a place in corporate learning; however, what I hope to do with this section is to provide a few fresh ideas for how you can leverage your leaders' wisdom in a way that appeals to today's learner outside the classroom.

Mentoring Circles

The first variation of LAT is called mentoring circles. Select two senior leaders to mentor a group of eight or so mentees who are all at similar stages of development. The mentees can be all women, all men, or a combination of the two, depending on the focus of the mentoring. Likewise, the mentors can be the same gender, but in my experience having one male leader and one female leader brings nice balance to the conversations.

Meetings can be held in person every month for two hours over a period of six to eight months. Except for the kickoff meeting (which is more of a "get to know you" session and agreeing on how the group wants to work together), the mentees organize and facilitate all the sessions, so this is not a heavy lift for the senior leaders. The leaders' role is to share insights and lessons learned on the topic being discussed. Sample meeting topics could include:

» emotional intelligence
» leading in a global environment
» personal brand and executive presence
» business acumen
» conflict management
» strategic business skills
» influence and persuasion.

Mentees can take turns "owning the agenda" and decide how the meeting will be conducted. They may have everyone read a book or article or watch a TED talk as preparation. They may elect to invite a guest speaker for a portion of the agenda. Whichever way they want to introduce the topic is up to them. And then the circle will have a discussion. This is where the two leaders or mentors add their perspectives. Figure 7-1 offers a sample agenda.

FIGURE 7-1. Sample Agenda for Monthly Mentoring Circle Meetings

Part 1: Staying Up to Date	
Review of agenda	5 minutes
Member updates and action assignment updates • What is new and upcoming in work and personal life • Debrief on action assignment from last session (what worked well and what didn't)	25 minutes
Part 2: Learning Together	
Monthly leadership topic and personal story sharing (e.g., a panel, guest speaker, video, presentation, book)	60 minutes
Overview of business unit • One member shares information about their department and their current focus	15 minutes
Part 3: Close Out	
Action assignment • Assign one action aligned to today's topic to be completed before the next session	10 minutes
Wrap-up • Debrief what worked well and what didn't during today's meeting and confirm facilitators and topic for next session	5 minutes

While the mentees benefit from building a strong network and learning new perspectives, I've also heard that the mentors take away a great deal from the experience.

Leader-Sponsored Communications

Who doesn't love a good podcast? Why not ask your leaders to be a guest on an upcoming podcast episode? This works nicely if you or your organization has a monthly show with different guests each month. It allows you to share the questions you're going to ask them ahead of time so they can prepare their responses and stories.

Another option is to ask leaders to record a video on a particular topic. It doesn't have to be professional-grade quality. All you need is a smartphone or tablet. I've done a few of these myself. With global teams spread out around the world, the videos I created were intended to keep us in touch with one another and in tune with our priorities. It also gave me a nice opportunity to recognize specific people for their contributions. I always added something I recently learned or was working on that they may not have known about. I am a firm believer in being a lifelong learner and wanted to ensure I was walking the talk.

A third form of leader-sponsored communications is good old-fashioned email. Greg Freidman, VP of leadership and organization development at Paraxel shared with me their "Leader Rx" initiative. Once a month a different leader would send a short email with microbursts of information around leadership that was mobile-device friendly. Topics could include how to be authentic and rebuild trust following a company layoff, or the message could prepare the organization for upcoming performance development conversations. They could include links to TED talks, favorite quotes, or stories and experiences that the leader wants to share. It's an effective way of circulating the "voice of your leaders" and for employees to get to know a handful of leaders on a more personal level.

Action Learning

Action learning is all about doing real work by applying what you've learned in the classroom to a current business challenge. During the time I was at GE's Crotonville, most of our leadership courses included some form of action learning project. The LAT would present a real, pressing business problem. If the class was learning about strategy, for example, they would apply their learning to a real-world GE challenge, which might involve expanding one of GE's businesses in a given region of the world. Participants would be assigned to a five- or six-person team, travel to that part of the world, interview customers, competitors, and business leaders, and generate a recommended strategy based on their due diligence. Each team would then present to a senior leader panel, highlighting different ideas and strategies. The panel would test assumptions and challenge the teams on various parts of their recommendations. What a fabulous way for the company to get "free" consulting services from some of the brightest leaders in the company. Such an action learning project doesn't have to require global travel; it's even easier if you're all together in the same location.

You can even follow a similar process without the classroom. There are platforms available whereby you can post details regarding an internal project where you need support. Employees "apply" for a temporary extra curricular activity (usually with the permission of their manger). This can serve as a great opportunity for someone to explore a different part of the business, get exposure to different leaders, learn a new skill, and make a contribution to the business. It is essential, however, that you have a project sponsor, preferably a business leader who can provide coaching. The leader gets help with a project and the volunteer receives valuable experience and exposure to a leader they may not normally interface with.

Fireside Chats

Fireside chats were one of my favorite applications of LAT from GE and Deloitte. They can be held as standalone events or in conjunction with a program. I always looked forward to the end of the day when we might have a reception with adult beverages being served. We would gather the participants around a real fireplace or an imaginary one (easy to get creative with a tv screen or computer monitor). The leader might start out by sharing a summary of their career and lessons they've learned along the way, or the challenges they are currently facing or have faced in the past roles. Many of the participants are usually in a reflective mood while listening so the leader gets asked some pretty powerful questions. This is when some of the most vulnerable discussions have taken place and leaders have opened up about stories that may not be well known across the organization. We can learn so much not only from our own failings but from the experiences of others.

Peer Coaching

LAT applications don't have to be about a single leader. Leaders can learn from each other. Bill George, professor of management practice at the Harvard Business School and the former chairman and CEO of Medtronics, made True North groups popular in his book, True North Groups; A Powerful Path to Personal and Leadership Development. He and his co-author, Doug Baker, have been practicing True North groups since 1975 and describe the experience as nothing short of a godsend in helping them navigate personal and professional challenges, addressing some of life's most difficult questions about their values, beliefs, and the meaning and purpose of their lives.

I have implemented peer LAT coaching groups as a supplemental experience in some of the leadership programs I've conducted. You typically have to be more prescriptive during the first couple of meetings, but your main objective is to have people get to know one another and slowly begin the process of being vulnerable with one another. If they participated in a 360 assessment prior to joining the group, for example, you may want them to share one of their strengths to the team and one area of development. Once the group has met a few times, they can usually create their own ongoing agendas. As they become more comfortable with each other, they will also become more candid with their observations and feelings. Peer coaching groups can be an effective way for your leaders to receive encouragement and reinforcement in terms of trying out new leadership approaches and behaviors.

You'll also discover a strong bond being formed within the group. Members will start calling on one another as they face challenges with their teams or projects. They will be more willing to admit if they are struggling with something and to ask for advice or assistance from one of their peer coaches. Many of the peer coaching cohorts formed will last well past the formal program as friendships emerge and trust grows stronger by the day.

Conclusion

Whether you've implemented an LAT approach in your business or are just starting out, the benefits speak for themselves in terms of not only attracting and retaining top talent but also ensuring your learning organization maintains a strategic alignment to the business. I hope I've convinced you it's worth building upon your initial momentum or beginning the journey of LAT. I've highlighted a few ideas but know there are many more out there that are just as compelling—there is no one right way. You can be as creative as you want to be with how you end up using your leaders.

Good luck to you and I'd love to hear about your experiences and new ideas. If I can be of any assistance, don't hesitate to reach out to me on LinkedIn.

8

Do More With Less: Using Your Budget Wisely

Michelle Braden

> You don't have to spend the most money to have an exceptional learning organization. It's about being efficient and effective with what you have.

One of the most common misconceptions in the learning industry is that the success of a learning organization is associated with the size of the learning spending budget. That the larger the budget, the better the learning strategy. But that's wrong. It is not the size of the learning budget that matters; it is what the learning organization does with what they have. Even though the latest reported industry average spending is approximately $1,299 per employee, many learning organizations' budgets are well below that (ATD 2019). However, all is not lost if you fall into that camp. A lower budget often forces innovation and creativity to provide the most value to the organization. All of which, if done well, will enable an award-winning learning strategy.

The learning industry is so advanced today and so full of such a large variety of solutions, tools, content libraries, and consultants that it can be confusing as to where to direct the limited learning spend. There is a temptation to sole-source to one vendor or one solution to make it easier. However, while easier, it is often not better and won't necessarily satisfy all the company's learning requirements and needs. Award-winning strategies are those that use a combination of in-house and outsourced learning solutions, content, and tools to maximize value to their organization.

Often due to a sense of urgency to provide learning solutions, many learning leaders succumb to the urge to obtain solutions and content before finding out what will bring the most value to the company. While it takes time to do the research into what is needed and what will be the most beneficial to the company and the employees, the payoff is tremendous. In this chapter, I'll cover some quick-hitting topics you should consider for your learning organization, with a focus on how to do the most with less.

Know the Business

No award-winning learning strategy started without knowing the business it was to support or understanding any pain points that existed. Conducting a bit of triage and speaking to executives and business leaders will tell you most of what you need to know. Put on your consulting hat and start by finding out what the critical success factors are for the business.

Ask:

» What would make your business area more successful?

» What is missing?

» What are the critical roles in this area for today and in the future?

» What skills are most important for those critical roles?

» What skills gaps exist today?

» Who in the business area is a role model for the critical skills?

The answers to these questions will provide valuable insight into the business area and its needs.

After collecting all this data from multiple business areas, compile it into an enterprise overview that illustrates the various needs and where they are located. Find the common threads across the organization. Determine where the greatest need exists that if addressed would provide the greatest value to the overall organization. There may be a common gap that exists across the organization—perhaps in the management population or maybe in a large functional area. Create a mind map, heat map, or other graphic illustration to show the extent of the needs.

During this step, it is easy to fall victim to concentrating on just one population or area because it is the one with the highest visibility. Don't. Your potential solutions for these areas, while viable, may not be the best to drive the greatest value. Therefore, the next step is to prioritize your efforts.

Prioritize Your Efforts

Successful, award-winning learning strategies don't address just one area of the company. They are typically multi-pronged and address many areas in a phased approach.

For example, at TELUS International, our triage exercise uncovered that the greatest need was to lower attrition and raise employee engagement of the global workforce during rapid growth. Subsequently, our root cause analysis determined that the fast growth had required employees to be placed in frontline team leader roles before they were fully trained, thus resulting in all learning occurring on the job rather than supported in the classroom. This led us to embark on a two-part solution.

Part One

To quickly address the resounding skills gaps, the first part of our learning strategy required developing an accelerated management development program and deploying it to the 1,000 current frontline team leaders. Because we worked with subject matter experts, we were able to develop our own best-practice content and utilize the handful of facilitators we already had located around the globe, thereby requiring very little investment.

Part Two

Simultaneously, we began working on the second part of our learning strategy, which was the design of a comprehensive multistage emerging leader's development program to prepare new frontline team members before they became frontline team members. With the rapid growth, we determined we needed to develop 300-plus frontline team members per year. To design this content, we interviewed several high-performing frontline team leaders and their managers to identify the key skills needed for success and used that as input into the design and development of a blended learning program incorporating already existing e-learning content, knowledge tests, instructor-led sessions, on-the-job activities, and guides for the participants' managers to support their learning.

Prior to graduation from the program, each participant was required to take part in a certification process confirming they were ready for a potential promotion to a team leader role. The certification included a final exam, presentation on the importance of good leadership, and a panel interview with business leaders, human resources, and the training team. Even though this program was done with very little investment, it has been recognized with several industry awards.

Once this program was completed and deployed, the accelerated program was no longer needed and was removed from the learning portfolio. This helped us make room for developing the rest of the strategy.

Keep It Simple

Don't fall victim to thinking the more complex the learning strategy is, the more effective. It isn't. That's the beauty of being forced to be innovative and creative with a lower-than-average budget. Keep it simple—focus on what will achieve the greatest impact. The simpler the strategy, the easier it is to explain, maintain, and refine. Keep in mind that employees want to know what they need to learn to perform at a higher level in their current role and prepare for their next role. And, don't resort to outsourcing this part of the work. Often, if you hire an external firm to create your strategy, you are going to wind up with something you cannot afford to implement.

At TELUS International, we created a powerful yet simple and award-winning multi-program career path called Learning@TI Roadmap to define how a team member could develop themselves to advance their career through four different career levels: individual contributor, manager of a team, manager of managers, and manager of organizations.

After we had the basic framework designed for the learning strategy and a few successful programs developed to address the most urgent needs, the next step was to socialize and refine it with stakeholders to ensure we truly understood their problems, skills gaps, and whether this strategy would address them.

What started with a mandate to build a leadership pipeline became a robust, comprehensive strategy with three primary objectives:

» Support team members in their current role by providing learning that will help them perform at their highest level and be successful.

» Proactively prepare team members for their next role before being promoted.

» Future-proof the company by maximizing the impact of learning and development.

These objectives required a solid yet simple vision and mission, which remained the same for over six years:

» **Vision:** Deliver extraordinary business value and customer experience through an exceptional continuous learning experience, enabling the best equipped, most highly skilled people in our industry.

» **Mission:** Strategically transform the way people learn and grow at TELUS International.

With a simple strategy, simple objectives, and simple vision and mission, it was relatively easy to maintain and evolve the overall strategic offerings. If it had been more complex, we would not have achieved the success that we did.

Continue to Evolve

The concept of developing team members before their next role became a critical element of our strategy.

After the first couple of successful phases, socialization with stakeholders, and some strategy refinement, we were ready to address the next challenge—onboarding new-hire call center team members before they started supporting our clients and their customers. While TELUS International's clients provided training relative to the business, products, or solutions the team members would be supporting, we needed to ensure that each new hire started with a good foundation to provide the best customer service possible.

Through extensive design thinking workshops with current team leaders and frontline team members, we were able to design and develop the IEvolve New Hire Foundations program to ensure that each new hire was set up for success with foundational customer service skills such as active listening, building customer rapport, and problem solving. This program, once deployed, demonstrated its value by improving customer satisfaction scores as well as reducing new hire voluntary attrition.

In addition, as part of the evolution, we decided to add a continuous learning element to our portfolio of solutions. However, with a minimal learning budget of less than $100 per employee, we had to stretch our innovation and creativity to find economical ways to not only broaden our portfolio, but also extend our reach across the entire global organization. So the Learn & Grow portfolio was born. It included five different learning modalities and sub-portfolios—including those that became the most popular elements of our entire strategy: videos and leadership talks.

The videos, which helped team members get to know our top leaders on a more personal level, were interviews with many of the top 100 leaders about their leadership philosophies, career paths, and learning lessons. A person on my team shot the videos using a camera and sound equipment and edited it with Adobe software we purchased. Today, it is very easy to make and edit videos in-house.

The leadership talks were in-person sessions, much like TED talks, with a team member sharing their insights, tips, and ideas about a variety of topics—some business-related and some not. Examples of session titles include "How to Find Your Mojo," "Three Keys to Your Success," and "Regain Your Work-Life Balance." The learning team interviewed the leaders while filming and subsequently editing the videos. They also worked with the speakers for the leadership talks to create and practice their session prior to delivery.

It was after seeing the success of these programs that we were finally awarded a nominal budget, although still much lower than the industry average. Consequently, we used every penny as creatively as possible. This leads to the next tip for watching where you're spending.

Mind Your Budget

With varied learner preferences and different settings and devices for consuming learning today, learning leaders need to mind their budgets and decide what to build, buy, or license. At TELUS International, our portfolio was a combination of many different learning modalities: instructor-led, e-learning, microlearning, video, simulations, mobile solutions, and more. For learning to be the most effective, it must be done in a variety of ways with the same or similar content. Not everyone will learn effectively from an instructor-led class. Some learn better with e-learning or simulations, and vice-versa.

Some content was licensed, some was purchased and re-branded (with permission, of course), and other content was created in-house. Our precious budget was reserved for licenses and content that could not easily be created in-house due to the lack of subject matter expertise required. Plus, there was no reason to build generic soft skill content because third-party learning libraries, created by industry subject matter experts, for both instructor-led and e-learning content could be purchased off-the-shelf for very little cost and rebranded with minimal effort.

To minimize facilitator costs while maximizing impact, we conducted train-the-trainer sessions with our in-house facilitators and leaders. We found that for certain courses, the facilitation was far more effective and impactful when leaders delivered them because they could enhance the delivery with business relevance, which in turn made the training programs much more attractive. An added benefit to this leaders as teachers tactic was the exposure and visibility the leaders received, thus increasing their personal credibility significantly (see Jayne Johnson's chapter 7 for more information).

While facilitated sessions were extremely popular, we quickly realized that to maximize our budget even more, we needed to leverage technology without losing the interactivity and key elements that had afforded our learning so much attractiveness to our team members and leaders.

Leverage Technology

In global organizations where the reach is vast, it is difficult to do much without technology. However, being selective about technology and how it is used can make all the difference in its impact.

In today's environment, very few companies have foregone the use of learning management systems (LMSs). Yet, with so many other options, it seems many more are omitting them from their technology landscape. Not too many years ago, the only way to use e-learning content was to have it stored and managed by an LMS. In fact, companies purchased content libraries and either stored the content in the LMS's content server or used the administrative function for managing the content on an external server.

Today, with a growing number of SaaS learning content providers, there is a diminishing need for the LMS as a storage platform. Yes, the LMS can still manage the content in learning paths and provide required reporting for mandatory and compliance training. Many of the newer LMS platforms now provide features that the older platforms did not. With a limited budget, it makes it even more important to do the research and look for innovative, economical, and more effective ways to manage learning content and reporting. Here are some important things to consider when trying to maximize your learning budget, especially since the majority have pricing models based upon the number of seats or employees it needs to serve:

» Does the platform have course authoring tools?
» Is the pricing by head or enterprise?
» Does it include career-pathing capabilities?
» Is it cloud-based (SaaS) or installed on premise?
» Does it integrate with your human capital management platform?

A few years ago, learning experience platforms (LXP) became popular. Utilizing machine learning and artificial intelligence, LXPs provide opportunities to the learner to access content that the provider curates, aggregates, and presents to the employee, based on their interests and skills, to enhance their learning experience. The content is typically from a variety of providers and includes courses, videos, e-books, podcasts, blogs, and articles. Some of the LXP's third-party providers require a subscription if not included in the portfolio of the LXP. Nonetheless, this can be an economical and effective way to provide access to a plethora of learning content without the added costs of individual license fees. LXP systems also include a social learning element enabling content rating, sharing content, assigning content, and commenting on content, while providing reporting and analytics to track the subjects and types of content learners are accessing. This information becomes important when making learning content portfolio purchasing decisions.

At TELUS International, one way we used an LXP was for our mid- and senior-level leaders to provide performance support in the flow of their work. Whether they had two minutes, two hours, or two days to learn something, they could start with the LXP to direct them to the most effective and relevant learning content. At WEX, we use an LXP for our entire enterprise to enable employees to find, access, and share relevant learning content to help build their skills and knowledge and ultimately grow their career with the company.

Other technologies that are useful in building successful learning strategies include those for web and video conferencing, online meetings, and webinars. Again, this is another market segment that is full of providers who have solutions fitting a variety of needs and budgets. At TELUS International, we used an online meeting or webinar solution to conduct live online sessions as part of the Learn & Grow portfolio. These were reserved for sessions that needed to be quickly deployed globally. To make them as effective as possible, the training team would moderate the session while a subject matter expert (SME) served as the primary presenter. The solution we chose included a host of special functions such as breakout rooms, whiteboards for collaborating, and polling to enhance the interactivity and engagement during the sessions. This is a very economical way to reach a larger audience, especially for content that has a short shelf life and thus requires frequent updates. Of course, you can use it for more permanent content and record the sessions for insertion in learning paths for playback.

While you are focusing on technology, don't forget the technology the learning team uses to design, develop, manage, and deliver curriculum development projects. At TELUS International, we used a variety of course development tools, project management suites, and interactive devices in classrooms and learning labs. On a per-license fee basis, these tools are not cheap; however, compared with outsourcing curriculum development, they are quite cost effective.

Market Your Solutions

Once you've used available and new technologies to design and develop your learning solutions, it's time to turn your attention to how you get the word out about them. But marketing isn't just about sending out e-mail blasts and hanging posters. It is letting employees and managers know what is available, putting it into their workflow, and showing compelling reasons to participate in the learning.

Several years ago, while at SAP, the online third-party e-learning library we had purchased for employees resulted in one of the highest participant uses as compared to the vendor's other clients. The success was due primarily to the marketing campaign we had created and executed to drive utilization. Rather than focusing on emails and posters, we took a multi-pronged approach to capturing the mindshare of our employees. After conducting focus groups to determine why learning and career development were important to our employees, we used their feedback to create slogans that would appeal directly to them. Using the slogans, we purchased and customized inexpensive learning swag and giveaways, such as earbuds, pens, notebooks, and mints to advertise the learning library. At large employee gatherings and during road show events, we handed out our giveaways. Employees loved receiving them and they were constant reminders about the learning library. To drive even more traffic to the library, we met with leaders and had them insert deep links to relevant learning in their emails and announcements.

At TELUS International, we created videos with testimonials from people who had participated in our programs. Then, we played the videos all throughout the buildings on flat screen TVs. We even put posters on the elevators and the stair risers in the stairwells. Our team created a set of graphics to be used on marketing materials and learning swag. Then, each region set about creating gadgets and giveaways like lanyards, desk accessories, and t-shirts that were reserved for program participants. We also worked with HR to make some of our programs mandatory for a promotion, which is excellent for driving awareness. And finally, we cultivated several executive learning champions, including our CEO, who would regularly talk about the importance of learning and encourage the leaders to support it. Don't expect them to talk about the actual learning solutions though. They would rather focus on the impact that learning has on the business results. That's OK, as it creates a more compelling reason for employees to participate and their managers to support their participation.

Evaluate for Effectiveness

To help leaders talk about the impact, it is important to create and maintain a meaningful dashboard to show who has participated and what the impact has been on their performance and business results. Investments in analytics tools and capabilities will help prove your business impact, which is critical to the success of any learning strategy. And, while measuring business impact is one of the most complex activities in creating an award-winning learning strategy, the results are well worth the effort.

Getting deep into performance and business results is paramount in proving your value to the organization. By measuring the performance and business results of individuals who attended certain programs against those who didn't, you can see the actual impact of the learning on the business.

At TELUS International, it took us months to determine what data to look for, where to pull it from, how to determine its accuracy, and how to create meaningful reports and dashboards to show the actual business impact. It was a complex undertaking. Our final dashboard showed analytics data from four different resources. It told a great story!

When we finally presented the dashboard to our senior leaders, proving that employees who participated in our programs had met or exceeded their business results and performance targets, demand for our learning programs increased. Plus, including these impressive business impact results helped us increase our CLO LearningElite ranking by 26 points to number 8 in 2019.

Develop Your L&D Team

While making the journey of creating an award-winning learning strategy, it is easy to get caught up in building and delivering to the point that you forget about your learning team. It is important that you continue to focus on them and their development. They need to stay abreast of the latest learning trends and continually improve their instructional design, curriculum development, performance consulting, and facilitation skills.

At TELUS International, we designed and built a robust development program for our learning and development team using ATD's Capability Model and competencies as a guide. The progressive, three-level program included a level for trainers, one for facilitators, and another for consultants. Each team member across the 400-plus team of trainers and facilitators worldwide was assessed by their manager and placed into the appropriate level as a starting point. From there, they began the program, which was built in-house using a combination of custom content along with our LXP's learning pathways feature as a guide. As they progressed, they were required to pass a series of toll gates to move to the next level.

The instructional designers, curriculum developers, portfolio managers, and learning technologists on the team participated in a variety of ATD courses and other industry programs to hone their skills, increase their knowledge, and gain industry certifications.

Each learning team member was also required to participate in the Learning@ TI Roadmap programs. To further enhance their career opportunities and movements, we also implemented a job rotation and shadowing program for the L&D team members.

All of this was done to not only provide a career path for our learning organization team members, but also ensure we were future-proofing our capabilities for the company as new digital services and technologies were introduced.

Continue the Momentum

It is critical that you and your team do all that you can to keep your learning solutions relevant and fresh to ensure that employees continue learning and growing. You need to continue to refine your strategy and content to ensure they are still supporting the business or solving problems or improving performance. You will also have to evaluate what is needed to support the company's future direction. If the corporate strategy has changed or evolved, yours also needs to change or evolve. Maybe conduct some more focus groups and design thinking workshops with team members and leaders from various business areas to gather their ideas for improvement.

At this point, you probably have technologies that are working very well for your strategy. However, depending on how long it took to create and execute your strategy, there could have been interesting advancements in technology that would be beneficial to your team or the greater organization. Speak to learning technology vendors to stay abreast of the latest technological advances in the industry.

Support your team and encourage them to continue their development. Perhaps now is the time to implement some job rotation for your learning team to expand their capabilities. They need to continually hone their skills and knowledge and grow as learning professionals.

And, take care of yourself. Participate in industry events. Expand your network. Read, research, talk to people, attend conferences, evaluate various learning solution providers, and stay in tune with what is happening in the industry.

Final Thoughts

As you are creating your strategy, you will probably run into some critics. Yes, you need to listen to their input and feedback. But it is important to apply critical thinking to ensure that you are not being swayed by bias or skepticism against the value of learning. Be forthright and try to persuade even the most fervent detractors. Better yet, see if you can convert them into champions for the cause. The more champions you have, the more the business will embrace your learning strategy and offerings, thus spreading the word faster about the great work you and your team are doing.

You don't have to spend the most money to have an exceptional and strategic learning organization. It's about how you use the funds you do have to build an efficient and effective learning strategy. And, to be efficient and effective, it doesn't need to be complex. Start simple by knowing the business, analyzing the challenges you need to solve, and then prioritizing where to focus your efforts and budget for the greatest business value. Don't spend your budget on content your team can create, but rather save it to license critical third-party content. When it comes to technology, do your research. You may not need all of the bells and whistles—instead determine exactly how you will use the technology and the value it will provide to the organization in driving your learning strategy. And, finally, focus on your team and their skills. The stronger they are, the more you can leverage their skills and knowledge to create an amazing and award-winning strategy.

9

Impact Matters

Martha Soehren

Turn measurement data into usable insights to prove the talent development function's impact on the organization.

Today's talent development (TD) professionals have a vast array of data available to them, and the importance of telling the story of impact on the business has never been greater. This is directly correlated to the role of the learning leader to manage talent development as a business. While talent development is generally a support organization that brings in little revenue, if done right, it can affect most revenue that comes into an organization. It makes great sense that more rigor is being applied to showing talent development's impact on improving the business across metrics.

The types of available data TD professionals need to drive business impact continues to evolve and increase over time. The data generally falls into two major categories: transactional learning data (the operational data we use to manage the function) or business metrics data. More and more, there is also data that occupies a middle ground, giving us insights into critical enablers of business performance (Figure 9-1).

There are the traditional sources of learning data such as the number of learners participating, the average class size, the minutes to complete a digital learning asset, and hours spent in a classroom. And there are the business indicators like cost, revenue, and customer satisfaction. In the middle ground, learning leaders might find things like participation in talent acceleration activities, a net promotor system, employee engagement data, retention data, and promotion data. Transactional TD data and business metrics data are both required for telling complete TD business impact stories.

FIGURE 9-1. Talent Development Metrics and Business Metrics

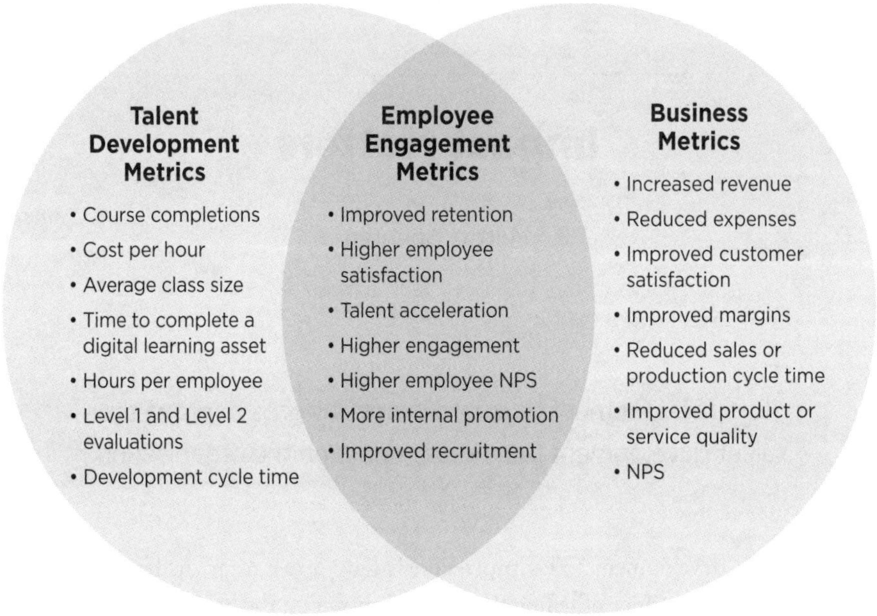

Talent Development Metrics

- Course completions
- Cost per hour
- Average class size
- Time to complete a digital learning asset
- Hours per employee
- Level 1 and Level 2 evaluations
- Development cycle time

Employee Engagement Metrics

- Improved retention
- Higher employee satisfaction
- Talent acceleration
- Higher engagement
- Higher employee NPS
- More internal promotion
- Improved recruitment

Business Metrics

- Increased revenue
- Reduced expenses
- Improved customer satisfaction
- Improved margins
- Reduced sales or production cycle time
- Improved product or service quality
- NPS

As data sources have become more readily available, TD professionals are including more business performance data to show learning impact against business key performance indicators (KPIs). Some organizations are putting a wrapper around transactional learning data and business performance data and leveraging data intelligence experts to help TD professionals predict the value of and show repeat employee performance against learning solution consumption. Companies leveraging predictive analytics are finding ways to better act upon talent and skills gaps for their organizations. This data is further enhanced by the growing sophistication of human resources information systems that link employee activity to skills inventories to drive adaptive learning by using deep machine learning in the HR space. This is the newest way in which the TD function is showing impact: driving critical decisions that make the organization perform better.

TD executives and learning leaders are feeling the need and taking the opportunity to use more meaningful measures to make sense of this ever-growing body of data. According to PwC's *15th Annual Global CEO Survey* (Church, Lambin, and Yu 2012), of the 80 percent of CEOs who say they need talent-related insights to make key decisions, only a small portion receive that information. A new data landscape requires an enlightened TD function—driven by a more rigorous and evolved approach to measurement.

Measurement is no longer just about proving the TD function's worth. Rather, it is about enabling the organization—and especially TD leaders—to maximize the value that the TD function provides. This is a rewarding time for TD professionals to show they are building and aligning their work to what is most important to the business. The data muscle needed to build and show the impact of learning solutions can be bought, borrowed, or grown within the TD function. Buying and borrowing data capability is easy and sometimes expensive. Growing or developing the data muscle within the TD function is harder and more time consuming, but has a bigger payoff.

Build the Data Muscle for TD Professionals

Organizations that grow the data muscle or data capability of their TD team have an advantage over those who buy this capability. Trainers, designers, and program managers work closely with the business in all phases of the ADDIE model (analysis, design, development, implementation, and evaluation), and are therefore closest to the business performance in their functional area as well as their market. Data capability across the TD organization makes for astute TD professionals who can tell the impact of learning solutions—a story at a time.

The analysis and implementation phases require the deepest application of data capability. When engaging with a business partner during the "what we're solving for" discussion, a TD professional who understands how to develop and set the stage for an impact story has an advantage when showing success with impact.

Formal training that helps TD professionals build their data muscle includes these topics:

» how to develop a survey instrument
» how to measure the cost and impact of administering a survey to a sample or population within the business
» how to assess results of a survey and use the results to prepare a question set for follow-on focus groups
» how to collect business performance data against KPIs for staging the impact story
» how to use learning and business data to develop the impact story
» how to present the impact story to the business
» all types of needs analyses:
    ◦ organizational analysis
    ◦ process analysis and mapping
    ◦ job and task analysis
    ◦ performance analysis
    ◦ requirements analysis (analysis of documents, laws, and procedures applied on the job)
    ◦ cost-benefit analysis

» data-gathering methods:
  ○ direct observation
  ○ questionnaires
  ○ consultation with people in key positions or with specific knowledge
  ○ review of relevant literature
  ○ interviews
  ○ focus groups
  ○ assessments and surveys
  ○ records and report studies
  ○ work samples.

It works well when this training is included in the development of TD professionals' career paths, making measurement an expectation across roles.

It's also important to give TD professionals ample opportunities to share their ROI and impact stories. At my company, we regularly share impact stories with business leaders, and we also provide opportunities for our TD professionals to share their impact stories with each other. Success with measurement drives more success with measurement—engaged TD professionals enjoy sharing the impact of their great work and learning from each other.

Workplace Transformations Drive New Thinking About Measurement

Two primary industry shifts are affecting measurement today and in the years to come. First, as described previously, data analytics is becoming an increasingly critical competency required of TD professionals. HR and TD functions are developing new and powerful tools to measure things they never could before.

I oversee the TD organization at Comcast Cable. Headquartered in Philadelphia, Comcast Cable is one of the largest video, high-speed Internet, and phone providers to residential customers in the United States under the Xfinity brand; it also provides these services to businesses. It also provides wireless and security and automation services to residential customers under the Xfinity brand.

Comcast's enterprise business intelligence team is partnering with the broader HR organization and the TD function to pursue meaningful predictive analytics studies. One of those we have on the timeline is to examine our 90-day onboarding process, which is self-directed and self-paced under an L&D professional's supervision. Through prior measurement, we've found that, in all cases, program results are better when an engaged peer mentor and supervisor pair with a trainer and learner. These new analytics will take the success story a step further by helping to predict retention and sustained performance for newly hired employees who have a dedicated mentor and supervisor. Our analyses to date show that, in most cases, new hires perform better than the average across all incumbents who perform in the same roles, when measured 30, 60, and 90 days after training. The next step for us is to predict sustainment post-participation in this type of learning environment. This will align with metrics such as retention and proficiency.

Today's open learning landscape is a second transformation driving new measurement thinking. At one time, "formal learning" was used to describe anything the training function designed and delivered; everything else was labeled informal. However, in today's workplace, learning doesn't have a consistent material form, and the classrooms, devices, and instructors that are used to give familiar substance to the process are only a tiny part of that landscape. Employees are finding and leveraging learning content from an abundance of sources. This learning is not informal. It is deliberate and often well-planned, not just by the TD function. The transactional data related to this learner-directed development is linked to touch points with a learning solution versus completions and time to complete. It allows learners to search for and find the specific content they need in the moment of need, rather than having to sift through and consume an entire digital asset or course that may also include content that is less relevant to them.

In a workplace where data are treated as a commodity and learning is taking place everywhere, the TD function must choose—strategically and intentionally—which learning solutions best show its impact. The following are four obligations for TD leaders who want to move beyond proving their transactional value to showing their business impact.

1. Become the Trusted Source

The TD value proposition reflects the company's concerns and values and drives the TD function's product and service portfolio. It determines a balance of facilitation, program administration, consultation, use of technology, design, development, and project management. It influences how the function approaches access, technology, customer interface, and cycle time.

Defining the value proposition drives critical decisions about the TD function's business and financial models, structure, and skill sets. The goal here is to be agile—quick to find, assess, select (or help others select), and implement (or enable others to implement) development resources. The end goal is to teach people to be their own trusted source.

Building a coaching culture is part of my TD team's value proposition. We are creating training content that helps frontline leaders and managers have the kinds of conversations that call out positive performance around KPIs. With business partners, we built this initiative, from analysis to implementation.

2. Measure What Matters

Every organization already measures what it thinks is critical, such as sales, cost per unit produced, contributions received, market share, quota attainment, or performance to plan. TD leaders should measure the success of development activities using the same metrics. At the start of each learning program, ask: What measurable business results will be evidence of success, and how best should we stage the measurement during design of TD solutions?

The TD function's primary responsibility is to be aligned with the business, for what's happening both in the short and the long term. TD professionals must be linked arm-in-arm with business partners, whether in the C-suite or the field, understanding what these individuals need. This close alignment during the analysis and design process permits the TD team to state the KPIs that will change the customer experience or business outcomes.

3. Measure Talent Development's Quality and Efficiency

While impact is the most important measure of how talent development is helping the organization, quality of service is the most critical indicator of the TD function's success. Every part of every company is obligated to improve over time. For example, employees should produce results more economically than last year, with reduced cycle time, better use of resources, and higher customer satisfaction. Done well, the TD function can routinely answer this question: How does the business know it is getting better at developing and delivering impactful results because of us? With the right metrics, TD leaders can be confident that their strategy is working.

The focus of this responsibility is to make sure that, if the organization is discovering new and better ways to get things done, agility is occurring as widely and thoroughly as possible—learning and failing fast is essential to success. It is the TD function's emerging role to help create and support networks that share developmental resources.

It is helpful to the TD organization as well as the business to design a TD transactional scorecard that can tell the story of instructor-led training (ILT) and digital consumption, Level 1 data for content and trainer delivery, and NPS scores for learning products and delivery, among other metrics. Figure 9–2 presents a sample dashboard for your consideration. Keep in mind, you'll want to send your business partners an updated dashboard at least quarterly and produce an annual dashboard for your annual report for the TD function. Going forward, new data analysis software will even make it possible for dashboards to provide real-time data on an ongoing basis.

FIGURE 9-2. Sample Transactional Dashboard: Making Learning Simple, Easy, and Digital

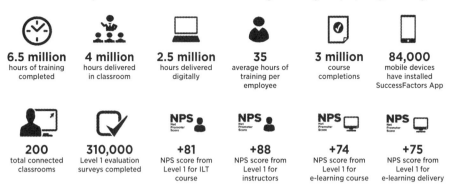

6.5 million hours of training completed	**4 million** hours delivered in classroom	**2.5 million** hours delivered digitally	**35** average hours of training per employee	**3 million** course completions	**84,000** mobile devices have installed SuccessFactors App
200 total connected classrooms	**310,000** Level 1 evaluation surveys completed	**+81** NPS score from Level 1 for ILT course	**+88** NPS score from Level 1 for instructors	**+74** NPS score from Level 1 for e-learning course	**+75** NPS score from Level 1 for e-learning delivery

4. Measure Individual Impact

In addition to how well the TD function meets organizational expectations, in the future the function must measure its impact on an individual's development. Individual impact expectations will likely fall into several categories:

>» Help me meet my training requirements.
>» Help me with training for my current job.
>» Help me with training for my next job.
>» Help me with a training plan for my career.
>» Help me identify training and nontraining options for my current job, next job, or career.
>» Help me figure out my career goals.

Increasingly, this personal focus will require TD professionals to measure whether each employee has a searchable development profile and report whether everyone has access to multiple virtual and physical learning environments. The TD function will be responsible for real-time measurement and monitoring of the activity stream—who is learning, where it is happening, and who needs help.

Making Meaning of Metrics

The ability to turn data into usable insights is at the heart of the new capabilities required of a future-looking TD function. To effectively measure where and how development is taking place, learning leaders and their teams should know how to analyze the organization, discover patterns, and document development.

Conduct an organizational cultural analysis. If working in teams is a fundamental organizational value, learning in teams is critical. If service is basic to the culture, then the tools for learning any number of skills for any number of roles must reflect a commitment to service. If inclusion, a global mindset, or innovation is deeply important to the company, then the approach to learning and the primary resources that support it must reflect those opportunities—and with formats and modalities that meet the employees where they are.

As organizations prepare for the workforce of the future, the ability to support a mobile workforce is becoming a priority. These individuals may never show up in a physical company facility. And because many customer interactions are also moving to the digital space, companies must ensure employees are prepared to interact with customers differently than they have in the past. To adapt to this change, companies must be prepared to hire people virtually, train them virtually, and lead them virtually.

Find the patterns. Patterns are important in data analyses. Understand what the company knows, what it needs to know, and when it needs to know it. Because learning is so fast, widely available, and individualized, the TD function should be the source of reflection on how and when the best learning happens. Search out simple patterns of learning needed and deeper patterns reflecting organizational culture and habit.

Document development. To see patterns in the organization, study what's happening. The future requires that the TD function embody the skills of development forensics—the capture, reuse, and modification of organizational learning capability. Such documentation begins by verifying that development has occurred and describing its results. Next, evidence acquisition, collection, and preservation provide proof that people learned from the development and, more importantly, that the perceived result made a meaningful difference in the organization.

The Role of a Governance Model in TD Measurement

A governance model is important not only to the TD function, but to successful impact stories. A governance model should consist of the most senior leaders in the business, co-chaired by the CTDO or learning leader and the senior business partner. The agenda should be strategic in nature and include ROI stories sprinkled in to show that governance decisions are making the intended impact. Figure 9-3 presents a diagram that shows how the national governance model at Comcast has worked since 2010. Note that membership evolves as the business evolves, always including the most senior leader from each functional unit, each business unit, and senior company leadership and the EVP of HR and the EVP of product.

The National Executive Learning Council is supported by functional advisory boards (we call them college advisory boards at Comcast) and geographically dispersed divisional delivery teams (which include the divisional operations presidents). This helps us align on business priorities, build the right muscle and capabilities, and show impact that drives an improved customer experience, ensuring the strategic direction of learning.

FIGURE 9-3. Sample Governance Model at Comcast

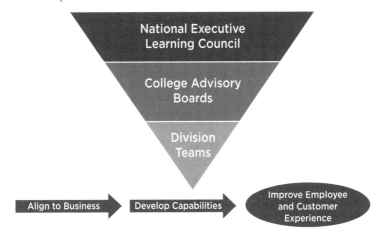

The Impact (ROI) Story

It is important to determine what is important for measurement upfront in the analysis phase of design and development. Figure 9-4 depicts a model we use at Comcast.

FIGURE 9-4. Connecting the Dots for an Impact Story

When engaging with a business partner on what it is that's being solved for (their business pain point), it's important to get a deep understanding as well as agreement on what the learning product is solving. In the process, agree upon the business metrics or KPIs that should be measured to see how the needle moved on those metrics 30, 60, and 90 days post-training.

The work then begins with the planning and building of the design of the learning solution. While in the plan-and-build phase, frequent engagement with subject matter experts from the business is critical, along with sign-offs from the executive business partner. Once the learning solution is delivered, regardless of modality, create the impact story.

The Impact Story Model Applied

Here is an example where this model was applied. It is an analysis for a learning solution that tackled a business problem where in one of our markets, a set of employees saw an increase in repeat troubleshooting tasks—and we fixed it! We used Kirkpatrick's Four Levels of Evaluation:

» Level 1: Reaction
» Level 2: Learning or Knowledge
» Level 3: Behavior
» Level 4: Results.

At Comcast, we always start by asking these questions: What are we solving for? Who is our executive sponsor? Who is the audience, and what are the business metrics we expect to evolve or impact? We used this approach to address the increase in troubleshooting visits to customers' homes. We started by analyzing the situation. We learned that troubleshooting skills needed to be strengthened.

Data used to analyze the situation in this market included:

» Review of business performance reports related to repeat visits to customers' homes.
» Analysis of the top 10 reasons for repeat visits.
» Conducting focus groups with field technicians and supervisors to further uncover the root cause of the pain point. It was important to include the field technicians, their bosses, customers, and call center agents in our data collection and analysis phase—they are our key stakeholders.

After addressing the pain point, we moved to the plan and build phase. We identified our key business metrics for this learning solution to be repeat visits to a customer's home to solve a problem after an installation of our products, and our "first-call resolution" metric, which indicated when the customer was cared for the first time.

Our data collection methods ensured alignment with business metrics, and budget implications were addressed up front. The metrics identified during the pain-point discussion were collected for a six-month baseline period. While doing this, we also negotiated up front with our business partners for easy access to post-learning performance data and reached agreement on a pilot market and a control group for measurement purposes. It was important to gain stakeholder buy-in here. This drove deep engagement with our field technicians and their supervisors, along with our business operations leaders and our senior business executive sponsor for the project.

The learning solution addressed troubleshooting skills with field technicians and their supervisors, the audience for the pilot learning solution. We built a blended learning solution that required supervisors to participate and partner with the field technicians. The learning solution tested the knowledge of the participants using a web-based troubleshooting solution that, depending on how the learner performed in the simulation, would show if the troubleshooting steps were done correctly or not, and equally as important, calculated the cost to the business when the troubleshooting was not done correctly.

We developed and implemented a blended learning solution—and here the directional improvements were impressive. Figure 9-5 shows how the cost to the business declined post-training with the pilot group. You can see that the control group, which received no training, drove a higher cost to the business for rework than the pilot group over this seven-month period. The business was so pleased with the outcomes of this learning solution that the savings were built into the budget for all markets for the following year, and all field technicians and supervisors were required to complete the learning solution.

FIGURE 9-5. Impact to Cost for the Trained and Control Groups

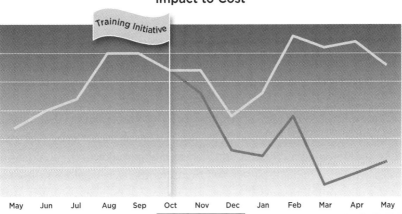

An Impact Story Using Learning Data Only

Using the impact story model, the business asked us to solve for the need to deliver a training solution to a group of employees on how we transport our signals through our network to our customers. These facilities are monitored by highly skilled employees around the clock and are generally very busy places.

The business pain point was simple: we needed a real-to-life learning solution to show our employees how things worked in this facility. We agreed to use augmented reality (AR) technology to build a learning solution that would give employees the feel of being in the facility as well as give them better troubleshooting skills.

We worked with one of our preferred vendor partners to build a learning solution that would give overviews of how signals and equipment work and are maintained, followed by a virtual tour. Our goal with monitoring learning data at the onset was to show whether there were efficiencies in using the AR solution versus the screenshot-based simulation. Here are the key findings:

» NPS scores were 81.7 for recommending the course and 83.3 for recommending the delivery approach.
» Learner responses showed they liked the modality, appreciating being able to see the equipment and visualize signal flows.
» 218 employees took the course with no risk to the facility by having employee tours.
» A tour takes an average of five hours (two hours employee time, two hours guide time, one hour travel time).
» The virtual tour saved nearly 800 employee hours (the course took more than 900 hours while the tour took just 109).

What's Next?

These new measurement requirements imply a host of competencies, both existing and new, for TD leaders and their teams to hone. They must have a better grasp of career development, coaching, job rotation, mentorship, and many other areas in which the TD function is involved, and to varying degrees depending on the organization.

TD leaders will need to ensure their teams develop greater skills in data collection, data analysis, and data visualization techniques. Their roles will require even greater skill in communicating business information to multiple audiences, social networking when supported by the business, and capturing user-generated content. Greater knowledge of statistical theory will be needed, along with the ability to select, design, and evaluate organizational research methods. In the next few years TD professionals will need to be able to move smoothly between descriptive, predictive, and even prescriptive analytics.

As we look at what competencies are needed in the Comcast workforce, we are moving much deeper into the space of people skills, interpersonal interaction skills, and relationship building. In an increasingly digital world, we are finding that social and communication skills are critical to support the ever-changing technological and digital landscape of the business.

In the final analysis, all the TD function's activities—its creations and discoveries, both for the organization's and individuals' development—are truly about talent readiness and optimizing the organization's performance. It is TD leaders' responsibility to take this strategic approach to measurement in the future TD function.

10

Collaborative Learning Drives Collective Ingenuity

Aimee George Leary, Ruth Almen, and Chris Holmes

> Collaborative learning triumphs over individual learning.
> To meet business-critical challenges, organizations need to
> embrace learning experiences that bring together diverse
> teams around a common purpose.

Award-winning learning organizations enable the purpose and values of the institution they support. They help the organization and its people build the confidence and skills they require to find the problem and solve it, be resourceful and creative, make the biggest difference, and harness the power of diversity. And they find ways to structure collaborative learning opportunities that can accommodate the pace of digital disruption and drive the collective ingenuity needed to empower people to change the world.

As we shift from the information age to the human age, and workers continue to perform tasks that automation cannot, transferrable and uniquely human skills such as creativity, empathy, and emotional intelligence become even more critical for organizations to develop. These human skills, which are seeded in peer networks, organizational communities, and teams, form the basis for the more human-centered approaches that will be required for workplaces of the future to effectively manage organizational systems that integrate automation and human performance. Additionally, as the workforce becomes increasingly more digital, diverse in demographics, geographically dispersed, and flexible (working away from a traditional office one or more days a week), organizations will rely more on collaboration to solve complex problems. Collaborative learning brings together diverse teams to embark on a shared experience around a common purpose or problem specifically designed to acquire new skills or knowledge. It's vital that learning organizations design opportunities for our people to learn through collective ingenuity.

The learning leader plays a crucial role in setting the stage for an environment primed for collaborative learning. To successfully apply it in your organization, you must take steps to ensure that the organization's culture and leadership is ready to accept and support the effort that will be required. A collaborative learning experience is one that needs to be curated from beginning to end, grounded in a culture that encourages and believes in continuous learning and is willing to focus on enabling and promoting learning behaviors as well as skills. As a learning leader, consider these imperatives as you design a collaborative learning experience:

» **Develop business intimacy.** Collaborative learning works best when teams are solving real and relevant business problems. Learners invest in the process wholly when they see their skills being applied to business problems that resonate. The organization must be willing to share real problems and internal challenges for learning opportunities. Your deep and intimate understanding of the business ensures successful application of the approach.

» **Establish commitment.** Business leaders must be committed to the philosophy of collaborative learning. Leader commitment to collaborative learning translates into personal investment of time and effort, and the willingness to let learners have the space and time to complete the experience. Your ability to create a shared organizational understanding of the value of collaborative learning is necessary to garner this collective leader commitment to the process.

» **Enable the infrastructure.** Dedicated teams that run collaborative learning programs require an organizational learning infrastructure (to include both resources and expertise) as well as individual team members with passion for providing the necessary learner support, program coordination, and a connected end-to-end experience.

» **Patience for getting it right.** Some collaborative learning programs can take years to mature, scale, or visibly yield a return on investment. The organization and stakeholders must be willing to have the patience to stay the course and cultivate outcomes over time.

The Collaborative Learning Framework

Booz Allen brings diverse perspectives together to solve complex problems for its clients—empowering people to change the world. We know that collaboration, diversity of thought, and the selfless service of our people, who lean in to help their colleagues every day, is the special sauce of our 105-year-old firm. These principles are explicit in our purpose and values, embedded in our leadership philosophy, and the foundation of our employee value proposition.

Our learning and development mission is to provide our people the essential knowledge needed to thrive in the Booz Allen environment, build the expertise of our technical and mission-focused talent, and develop the leaders of the future. Our learning programs provide clear access to the latest thinking, the latitude to learn how they prefer, and the pathways to apply their knowledge and skills to unlock new opportunities. Regardless of the area of focus, our learning programs are built around a Collaborative Learning Framework that reinforces the bedrock of our purpose-driven leadership and values-based culture—and specifically, drive our collective ingenuity (Figure 10-1). The framework combines key factors and approaches for enabling the development of human-centered skills within various learning programs.

We define this Collaborative Learning Framework through five core attributes:

» applied knowledge through solving real problems to a common purpose
» a structured approach to learning (which includes an intentional diversity of participants)
» a commitment to personal skin in the game (to include recognition and incentives)
» fostering connections (within the cohort and across the enterprise) to build meaningful networks
» an inclusive team construct where everyone can contribute, openly share their expertise and experiences, and learn and fail in a safe environment.

FIGURE 10-1. The Collaborative Learning Framework

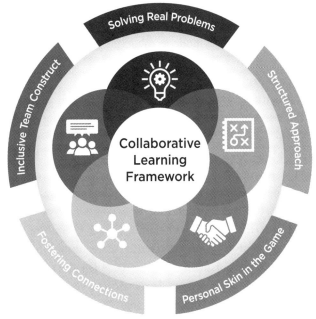

Because of this framework, we have seen improved retention, employee experience survey results, and promotion rates, as well as new business opportunities created, new products and solutions developed, greater leader readiness, new and deeper relationships established, and greater self-awareness, emotional intelligence, and political savvy within the organization.

In the rest of this chapter, we will share examples of how Booz Allen has applied the Collaborative Learning Framework in practice through different types of programs and development, all with successful and award-winning results. Tech excellence, hackathons, capture the flag events, and the summer games programs are examples of collaborative learning programs focused on building technical skills, problem solving, creativity, and interpersonal team skills. The Leadership Excellence program and learning circles are examples of leadership development programs that use collaborative learning to emphasize influence, empathy, emotional intelligence, and communication among other key leadership skills.

Tech Excellence

Tech Excellence is Booz Allen's repeatable model of upskilling and reskilling our people to meet the needs of a changing market while advancing their capabilities and investing in their growth. They are intensive, cohort-based programs that build capacity for in-demand skills areas. The programs comprise several components, including structured and applied learning, engagement with the team and experts, assessments to gauge progress and aptitude, and placement.

The current Tech Excellence model is the result of lessons learned over a period of years from several iterative approaches and programs. Key to their success is that the programs are not just training—they integrate these multiple components for a comprehensive, structured, and repeatable talent development approach. This highly effective model of learning results in 76 percent of learners being rated "highly proficient" in the skill area at the course's end.

Engagement is a significant factor in Tech Excellence programs, and opportunities for exposure are purposefully built in throughout each program. Participants need the encouragement and connection that comes from being a part of a team, even before joining that team. Managers and mentors play a key role during the multiweek program: Mentors meet weekly with participants in "mentoring circles" as well as one-on-one as needed, and managers are intentional about meeting with and getting to know employees throughout the program. Booz Allen also structures interactions with leaders and subject matter experts. Leaders often visit with the cohort in the form of "fireside chats"—informal discussions that allow participants to ask questions of leaders and gain an understanding of the culture and expectations. Subject matter experts provide a view into the industry they will be joining by sharing a day in the life experience and describing various expectations of the role and market.

Fundamental to the Tech Excellence programs is allowing participants the opportunity to solve real-world problems. Whether the program is focused on data science, cyber, or software development, participants are offered the opportunity to apply their skills to current client challenges. In the Tech Excellence Data Science program, employees work on and present a final capstone project to their cohort peers and leaders from the firm. They are challenged to solve real problems using open-source data sets. The applied learning capstone also provides participants an opportunity to be publicly recognized for their accomplishment and skills learned in the program. In fact, one of the leaders during a Data Science 5K Capstone presentation selected a participant to join their team solely on what they heard in the presentation.

Hackathons and Capture the Flag Events

Sometimes old problems need fresh eyes. Employees who work on the same client problems day to day can grow frustrated by a lack of progress, but there might be others with the relevant domain expertise or skill sets to develop solutions throughout the organization who are focused on their own client engagements. Identifying and convening the right group of people to tackle these challenges together is a worthwhile exercise that can also be time consuming and effort intensive. A key element of impactful learning is the participant's investment. Whether through their investment of time, energy, or taking risks in a safe environment, a fundamental component of successful learning environments is that learners are fully invested. Booz Allen has developed an internal tool and service offering that structures capture the flag (CTF) events to allow teams to build and apply cyber skills. In a capture the flag event, individuals form teams of up to three players to compete against other teams. CTF events can run for several hours, and sometimes even days depending on the complexity and structure of the event, leveraging cybersecurity skills such as networking, web, coding, forensics, reverse engineering, and exploitation.

These events create a fun and competitive environment that replicates a realistic scenario. A recent CTF plot was centered around a senior ranking government official's hospitalization, and teams had to defeat hackers who were attempting to gain access to the hospital's network to compromise the systems and authorize a lethal dose of medication to the government official.

For each event, challenge designers optimize milestones to structure recognition at stages throughout the CTF; shorter problems must be solved in approximately 20 minutes, allowing players to constantly feel challenged. Challenges are designed to accommodate all experience levels, providing more senior technical participants motivation to compete, test their skills, and gain points on a leader board and giving more junior participants the opportunity to trade points for hints, work with mentors, and research and learn how to solve problems.

CTFs can also highlight the importance of identifying individual strengths to maximize contribution in a team environment. The most successful CTF teams comprise individuals with diverse skill sets and experiences. These teams collectively identify their various strengths and apply them strategically to various parts of the problem—effectively dividing and conquering challenges to maximize their score. Strong teams must maximize communication and problem solving to most effectively apply their technical prowess. Teams learn in real-time that a lack of collaboration results in their being stuck on a problem for an hour or more of the competition, reducing the number of questions solved and their overall score.

"Capture the flag events require individuals to contribute wholly to the process," one Booz Allen Hamilton leader and cyber expert said. "The most effective and successful teams uncover and leverage each other's unique strengths throughout the process, requiring each individual to contribute at his or her highest level while relying on teammates to do the same."

Truly 100 percent hands-on, CTF events emphasize independent learning without lecturing. Mentors walk around and provide one-on-one help when needed, but participants are encouraged to succeed leveraging their teammates' skills and expertise.

Booz Allen cyber expert Garretson Blight helps design and structure CTFs for internal employees as well as clients. "Events such as CTFs can encourage collaboration, competition, and fun amongst participants," shares Blight. "Employees find CTFs both challenging and rewarding: CTFs require employees to learn on the fly and solve problems outside of their areas of expertise."

Summer Games

The Summer Games turns the traditional internship experience on its head. Participating interns are encouraged to collaborate and are given the intellectual freedom to develop and prototype ideas aimed at solving major world problems. Interns are grouped into teams, each led by a Booz Allen senior leader. Teams are then assigned a major problem to solve, based off a curated list of crowdsourced issues submitted by our employees. In the span of 10 weeks the teams meet, collaborate, and iterate solutions to their issues. Students learn new technical skills, network with innovative business and thought leaders, and participate in engagement events. In addition, students explore new areas and problems through the Student Incubator, where senior leaders and clients select the most promising ideas. Finalists return during the academic year to develop their idea into a proof of concept.

During the multi-week program, interns attend structured networking events outside work that allow them to develop relationships with one another as well as leaders and employees of Booz Allen. Through this experience the interns realize the importance that personal relationships and community membership play in the workplace and their overall success.

That work culminates in three *Shark Tank*–inspired pitch sessions in front of a panel of Booz Allen senior executives, where teams compete to win funding and benefit from mentoring to grow their idea. A previous winning team explored the problem of human trafficking and ultimately developed a sensor that could detect a human heartbeat within cargo containers.

In addition to the protocol for hiring the right type of students, the very structure of each challenge team fosters innovation. Each team is constructed to evidence three key traits: individual roles are collectively defined and assigned by the students, teams design their own solution and, with limited oversight from their challenge leaders, govern themselves. Leadership of each team is contextual and distributed among the interns as the work changes. This looser, more fluid structure facilitates creativity and innovation, resting on the support provided by the resources and structure of the larger program.

The Summer Games provides both top-quality junior talent to meet the firm's demands and creative, actionable solutions for a wide variety of current business clients. In addition, the program has also provided intangible results. Because of these measurable successes, the Summer Games has become something of a cult brand, recruiting top university talent who are optimistic, future-focused, and open to risk and change. The games experience serves as both inspiration and information, being a badge that gives them permission and encouragement to question the status quo and strive for creating a better world. As might be expected, it is the students who are the real innovators, mentored carefully by the challenge leaders.

Leadership Excellence

The Leadership Excellence Program (LEP) is talent management in action. Designed to strengthen the leadership pipeline by preparing exceptional high-performing and high-potential leaders to take on broader roles in the firm, this program is the corporate equivalent of a triathlon: intense, sometimes fierce, and always invigorating. Pushing themselves harder than perhaps they ever have in their careers, these leaders take on stretch assignments, engage with coaches, and through the Community Leadership Project (CLP), work in teams to tackle the challenges of a new client, a deserving nonprofit that is already doing great work—but that needs to up its game to thrive.

This multi-phased progressive development journey is a structured and comprehensive approach that attacks learning in multiple ways to create an intense, transformational leadership experience through components such as 360-degree assessment and feedback, one-on-one executive coaching, cohort residential sessions, and the community leadership project.

The Leadership Excellence Program begins with a structured informational webinar to ensure participants and their career managers are clear on program and participant expectations. To maximize learning and their commitment to the program, participants are required to review the expectations during this introductory session and sign both a commitment letter and statement of intent. This is one way we reinforce the importance of full participation in the program and gain agreement to the level of effort required. In completing the statement of intent, leaders reflect on their hopes for the program, their strengths, and areas for further development. This session then informs the design, learning strategies, and approaches used to deliver a powerful and robust learning experience.

The experiential component of the LEP, the Community Leadership Project (CLP), combines the dual purpose of significant community impact that serves as a catalyst for deepening leadership skills, expanding peer networks, and building relationships with project champions. The CLP is a complex, multi-month, team-based consulting engagement that truly provides a construct for actionable learning in an inclusive team construct. It allows leaders to collectively leverage their extraordinary technical skills and creates a safe place to experiment with newly learned leadership skills applied to a project that truly matters.

The CLP aligns each leader by area of interest to form diverse consulting teams. Throughout this project, leaders experience how to assume roles and relationships when collaborating with a team of high-performing peers—a skill that prepares them for the horizontal authoritative dynamics of working with senior leaders. In taking on new challenges, these leaders grow in their own leadership ability, give back to the community, and deliver to their clients.

Projects focus on real problems and challenges currently faced by select nonprofit community organizations. Project outputs may include deliverables such as competitive analysis, a reusable decision framework, a comprehensive execution plan, a SWOT analysis producing strategic goals, or a business plan and implementation road map. In all cases, the projects make it possible for community organizations to tackle otherwise seemingly impossible challenges due to lack of resources, time, or skill sets. These projects provide lasting impact and value to our community partners and the leaders and members of the local community. Our leaders' expertise strengthens nonprofits' capacity to perform by providing in-depth analysis and recommendations that inform strategic decisions and thus increase organizational efficiency and effectiveness.

From Booz Allen's perspective, this program is a huge success in developing our leadership pipeline. By design, the program pushes leaders into the unknown. Our leaders work outside their areas of expertise, collaborate with new clients on unfamiliar assignments, and engage with peers they have never worked with before. These stretch opportunities allow participants to share their expertise and experience through peer-to-peer collaboration and force them to exercise strategic thinking and leadership skills to solve new and diverse problems. This construct acts as a learning lab for leaders to deepen their skills while making significant community impact and expanding relationships inside and outside the firm.

Learning Circles

Learning Circles are small groups of peer-level leaders across the enterprise, including all areas of expertise, functional disciplines, tenure, and geographies. Although Learning Circles may appear to be an informal, casual opportunity to connect in a small group setting, their structure ensures they are a true collaborative construct for fostering connections through peer-to-peer, networked learning.

To start, there are several roles supporting a learning circle including a sponsor, a circle advisor, and a circle lead. The sponsor provides guidance on timely and relevant topics aligned to the business and engages periodically with circle advisors to share insights and gather feedback. The circle advisor is responsible for ensuring participants attend the quarterly meetings, and during each Learning Circle meeting they provide senior perspective, mentoring, guidance, and exposure to the participants. The circle lead works in partnership with the circle advisor and acts as a facilitator for discussions. The lead is also responsible for scheduling the meetings and planning and coordinating agendas and any logistics. Finally, the lead works with the leadership development program team to integrate priority topics into the meetings. Members of the leadership development team provide tools, content, and resources, as needed. Often, they share best practices and tips to drive a consistent experience across circles and conduct an annual survey to monitor quality and continuously improve.

Learning Circle groups are intentionally designed as mixed groups to promote diversity of thought, experiences, background, demographics, and cultures to offer leaders a chance to engage in thoughtful discussion, (at times) lively debate, and a broad range of perspectives that wouldn't ordinarily be available in their day-to-day interactions. Learning Circles meet in person on a quarterly basis throughout the year (using WebEx or Zoom, or physically co-located), with fierce dedication to attend. This commitment of personal skin in the game creates an unspoken expectation and drives the accountability for leaders to show up and contribute with sincerity and candor, no matter what.

Learning Circle topics routinely include discussion around firmwide priorities, critical business challenges, or aspects of development for leaders. Over time, a Learning Circle comes together and bonds both personally and professionally through candid conversations that tend to spark just the right amount of tension and difference needed to foster a mutual respect among participants even when their perspectives may differ on any given topic. The trust that participants build with each other is evident as leaders feel safe in sharing their expertise, personal experiences, and feelings without judgement. This cross-pollination of ideas extends beyond the Learning Circle as newfound ideas, ways of thinking, and possibilities help leaders carry forward new possibilities, solutions, and understanding to better serve our clients and their most critical missions.

How to Achieve a Collaborative Learning Experience

A first step to successfully applying collaborative learning in your organization is to ensure that your organization's culture and leadership is primed and ready to accept and support the effort that will be required. The collaborative learning experience is one that needs to be curated from beginning to end. This requires a learning culture that encourages and believes in continuous learning and is willing to focus on enabling and promoting learning behaviors as well as skills. Consider these factors before designing a collaborative learning experience:

» Willingness to share real problems or internal challenges for learning opportunities. The organization or teams must share problems and invest in the process with your learning and development team from the outset.

» Committed leaders who buy in to the philosophy of collaborative learning. Leader commitment must translate into time, effort, and the willingness to let learners have the space and time to complete the experience.

» Committed participants who see the value of learning programs. The most successful participants will not only be actively engaged in the process but also more motivated as their success is dependent on them.

» Dedicated teams to run collaborative learning programs. Learning experiences like these take an organizational learning infrastructure (to include both resources and expertise) as well as individual team members with passion for providing the necessary learner support, program coordination, and a connected end-to-end experience.

» Patience for getting it right. Some programs can take years to mature, scale, or visibly demonstrate the return on investment. The organization and stakeholders must be willing to have the patience to stay the course and cultivate outcomes over time.

As we developed and implemented each of these programs, we started to see common elements emerge that we captured into a design checklist. All the program examples shared here use the Collaborative Learning Framework and many of the design elements are integrated throughout. Not all programs need nor will have all elements, but to achieve a true collaborative learning experience you should incorporate several into your program design.

Collaborative Learning Framework Design Checklist

Solving Real Problems
Applied knowledge through solving real problems or common purpose:
- ❑ Source real problems and business challenges from teams, clients, or leadership that can be solved or worked on and will provide meaningful value to the cause.
- ❑ Identify case studies to learn from relevant issues and challenges that others have faced and overcome.
- ❑ Use the problem-solving opportunity to get the collective group to see a common purpose or outcome that applies to all.

Structured Approach
A structured approach to learning (which includes an intentional diversity of participants):
- ❑ Define a specific timeframe or cadence.
- ❑ Use multiple learning strategies and approaches throughout.
- ❑ Build diverse teams for learning (backgrounds, skills, divisions, roles).

Personal Skin In The Game
Commitment of personal skin in the game (to include recognition and incentives):
- ❑ Define the commitment up front (for both participants and managers) and gain agreement to the level of effort (such as a signed commitment letter).
- ❑ Create specific accountability checkpoints for individuals and the group or milestones reinforced with badges.
- ❑ Look for methods to build recognition into your program, whether it is a capstone event with leadership attendance or presenting solutions to stakeholders.

Fostering Connections
Fostering connections (within the cohort and across the enterprise) to build meaningful networks:
- ❑ Create fun internal and external social opportunities or team building to foster deeper relationships.
- ❑ Design ways for learners to share their expertise and experience.
- ❑ Engage leaders throughout the journey to open additional opportunities.

Inclusive Team Construct

An inclusive team construct where everyone can contribute, openly share their expertise, and learn in a safe environment:

- ❑ Establish "Vegas rules" or guiding principles to enable the psychological safety of the learning environment.
- ❑ Ensure everyone has a meaningful role, contributes, and is pushed beyond their comfort zone.
- ❑ Create learning buddies or trusted partners for candid feedback loops and encouragement.

11

Agile Is the New Smart

Laura Lee Gentry and Annmarie Neal

Old habits die hard. Learning leaders must actively lead their organization in the transformation to an agile learning culture.

Many organizations find it challenging to cope with the increasing pace and unpredictability of change, fueled by rapid growth and global scale, disruptive innovation, and the digitization of products, processes, and business models. The ambiguous, complex, and turbulent nature of today's—and tomorrow's—businesses demand that we reimagine how, where, by whom, and with whom business is done. In addition, it's clear that organizations can increase growth and productivity by empowering leadership and encouraging individuals to self-organize, while creating new and disruptive forms of value. Essentially, organizations find themselves needing to activate more innovation within their teams, with greater agility and fluidity, while capitalizing on new and disruptive technologies and social-structured networks. This will require a significant redesign of how work is organized, how leaders lead, and how employees—bought or borrowed—engage, learn, and perform. Extending to the talent development function, learning executives can no longer rely on traditional—and soon to be obsolete—organizational, leadership, and learning practices to drive culture and business impact.

We believe the foundational leadership and organizational disciplines in disruptive environments are similar to those required in more stable business dynamics, with a few notable exceptions. In this chapter, we will focus on the most notable exception: agility. The primary role of learning, organization development, and human capital executives is to strategically reimagine the organization so that ideas become the new product and agility becomes the new smart.

In this chapter, we hope to accomplish three objectives:

» Highlight the critical attributes of agile cultures and agile leaders.

» Showcase an agile organization and culture in action with a high-growth technology company: Ultimate Software.
» Share lessons from consulting with high-growth agile systems, teams, and leaders.

What It Means to Be Agile

To successfully compete in a disruptive environment amid unprecedented change in industries, markets, digital technologies, and social pressures, organizations must learn to how to be agile. Otherwise, they will be hard-pressed to accurately create and sustain positions of value.

Cultural characteristics of agile organizations include:
» Hyper-attentive in their anticipation, evaluation, and application of new and emerging trends to product strategy, customer experience, and value-creation initiatives.
» Hyper-collaborative to make corroborated decisions, break down silos, and drive large-scale change.
» Evidence-based, leveraging data to make informed decisions.
» Empowered by diverse teams with multifaceted skill sets and capabilities who address both current and future business needs.
» Clear of purpose and change-ready to capitalize on exciting new opportunities and challenges.

If an organization must be agile to compete effectively in disruptive environments, its leaders must be agile, too. But what exactly makes a leader agile? In *Leading From the Edge: Global Executives Share Strategies for Success*, Annmarie articulated the following characteristics that distinguish agile from non-agile leaders:
» An unusually astute sense of self, or an ability to understand the world and people on many levels and in many different contexts; current thought leaders now describe this as mindfulness.
» The capacity to rapidly absorb, synthesize, and organize information to determine how best to lead themselves and their organizations and nurture connections across industries, technologies, markets, and geographies.
» The intellectual acuity to know what to keep, what to destroy, and what to recreate to help their organizations remain relevant to many different markets and constituents.
» An inventor and experimenter mindset, willing to try out new ideas and hypotheses.
» An embrace of failure as a necessary ingredient to success; they understand, learn from, and recover from failure.

» The understanding that their organizations are part of living systems, in which the success of the individual is dependent upon the success of the larger whole.

» The skill to co-exist in two worlds: one where a certain level of control and oversight is required to drive performance expectations, and the other where they set the vision but allow those working on the edges to self-organize and find solutions—perhaps to problems that have not even been considered or experienced yet.

Most organizations don't wake up one day and become agile. Nor do most leaders or teams. Developing an agile culture and organization takes vision, strategy, courage—and smart execution. Let's explore how a strategic learning organization can leverage these agile characteristics to become a valued partner to the business. We'll use our company, Ultimate Software, as an example of one that embraces an agile, people-first culture to drive new forms of value through its people, culture, leadership, and learning practices. True learning organizations take great pride in their ability to evolve at the speed of the market.

Make People, Talent, and Learning a Business Imperative, Not Just an HR Initiative

Learning leaders need to make agility a crucial aspect of their people, talent, and learning strategies. This starts with asking the question: "What do our customers, people, and teams need to be ready?" Looking three to five years out, you will want to know how you to scale and adapt your business to ensure you can perform optimally today and as it grows in size and complexity. Your learning programs must ensure that your people can keep pace with the needs of the business and the markets in which you serve.

A high-growth technology company, Ultimate Software has been growing by 20 to 30 percent per year for the past 10 years. With this growth comes organizational and operational complexities. As a result, our people, talent, and learning organizations are exceedingly business-minded in all that we do and set out to accomplish. At the end of the day, our success is aligned to business and customer success. Embedded deeply in our operational teams, we are an equal partner to our leaders, and willing to challenge them on learning strategies. Our business and people, talent, and learning teams work side-by-side to ensure that all initiatives are designed and executed to address the company's most important business, customer, organizational, and people priorities.

Award-winning culture leads to award-winning innovation. Nucleus Research, a prominent analyst firm, deemed us a Leader in HCM technology. In 2019, Ultimate earned the Gold Excellence in Technology from Brandon Hall for Best Advance in Assessment and Survey Technology and Customer Service Department of the Year.

Because innovation and customer health are core to Ultimate's business, we are working on several new strategies we expect to drive our next phase of growth. These include incorporating emerging HCM technologies that will fuel customer success, continued international expansion and acquisitions, and heightened competitive intelligence. This rapid pace of expansion requires a balance between stability and adaptation as we prepare our people, teams, and leaders for continual growth and innovation.

Our people, talent, and learning organizations are aligned to strategically address:

» Recruiting, onboarding, and deploying culturally aligned, agile employees who are hungry, humble, and capable of growth.

» Developing our managers and leaders to successfully run the company while leading and driving our people-first culture.

» Empowering our team members and customers to perform their best both today and in the future.

» Preparing our people to embrace change as a natural course of the rhythm of the business.

» Leveraging our products' analytical power to rigorously understand our workforce dynamics, from skills and capabilities to career interests and employee sentiment.

In the rest of this chapter, we'll take a look at each of these priorities, what they mean for you, and what you might learn from our experience.

Priority 1: Grow Your Agile Team While Protecting the Culture

The challenge every company faces as it expands is how to grow without losing the culture they've already established. Here learning leaders have an important role in ensuring that new hires align to the culture. At Ultimate, we understand that our people are the business. Therefore, a key element of our recruiting approach is to protect the house. We accomplish this by attracting team members who truly embody and embrace our values, such as teamwork, collaboration, partner for life customer service, and servant leadership.

Learning leaders can look to dedicate resources to ensure that you attract and hire for culture fit and learning agility. Organized by division, our world-class recruiting team is embedded in the business and operates as trusted partners with deep relationships and credibility with hiring managers. They know the organizations they serve and thus can articulately and credibly speak to business and product strategy with top candidates. In this way, they are brand ambassadors and brand protectors.

Therefore, first and foremost, we screen for culture fit. Ideal candidate traits include strong, personal drive and a sense of urgency; team players who understand servant leadership; and strong emotional intelligence that enables them to connect with, draw out, and create trust with many types of people. Further, we leverage best-in-class assessment tools and methodologies to assess our managers and leaders on agility attributes.

In addition to hiring, onboarding matters deeply when growing your team. At Ultimate, our onboarding program engages new employees from the moment they sign their offer letter because we want to immediately express our appreciation for the value that new arrival brings. We deliver customized learning paths and support new hires with check-ins at the 30-, 60-, and 90-day mark. Our CARE (culture, awareness, relationships, and expectations) program layers in additional steps for new leaders so that they can understand Ultimate's high expectations of their new role and support rapid success. Finally, onboarding culminates in our two-day New Hire Event where executive leadership meets with new team members and shares their team vision.

Priority 2: Develop Leaders to Run and Grow the Company

Empowerment and accountability are very strong elements of an agile culture. Leaders and their people must feel empowered to make strategic and operational decisions within their remit and serve up ideas on how they can innovate or improve. Agile also means encouraging experimentation and following a "fail forward" model where new ideas are welcomed and tested. This starts with leadership.

At Ultimate, new team members come into a world of "how," not "if," and we reinforce that they are safe to try new things. Leadership has their back, and they know it. New ideas are piloted and observed closely with fast feedback loops to tweak and adapt. The result is game-changing new products, programs, and models for our customers, leaders, and team members.

Equally, we are data and insights driven, not only bringing actionable insights to business leaders but holding our programs accountable to true business impact. This was a very purposeful strategy to ensure our teams were grounded in the business. The unexpected and delightful outcome was the unparalleled team spirit that resulted: a rich, fruitful environment where our team members grow at an incredibly steep rate. We have earned the credibility of challenging the business to make the changes required for our continued success.

To ensure adoption of an agile, people-first culture, Ultimate understands that it needs to create the conditions for continuous learning, from our senior-most leaders down deep into the organization. To this end, we offer a few integrated programs:

LEAD US Series

Our flagship leadership development program has three modules, all designed to meet leaders where they are in their career. Module 1 is called LEAD US Footprints and is designed for our high-potential individual contributors who desire to be people leaders. Module 2 is called LEAD US Foundations and is designed for current people leaders who want to further develop their leadership skills and capabilities. Our third module is called LEAD US Forward and is designed for directors and vice presidents who wish to master their skills and capabilities as business leaders.

Each year-long program consists of eight six-week modules, with small breaks in between. The programs are designed to balance knowledge depth with the practical realities of a full-time role. Each employee works through the program as a class, connecting leaders from all parts of the business and fostering cross-functional understanding. Kickoff and graduations take place in-person with participation from senior leaders. The class works together virtually throughout the rest of the year, leveraging collaboration software and our social learning platform, UltiPro Learning.

Each module incorporates two weeks of reflection and application to deepen retention and ensure insights are applied to participants' day-to-day work lives. A 360-degree assessment on 42 behaviors linked to our leadership competencies is conducted both prior to starting and upon finishing the course to measure specific, relevant behavior growth. The program has been an enormous success, reflected in our ready-now succession pipelines, employee retention, talent progression, and My Manager and Team Health scores in our employee surveys.

Technical Track

Not everyone is destined to be a people leader. Any company that has subject matter experts (SMEs) in their employee population needs to be wary of creating an environment where the only path up is to become a people manager. We developed and deployed a technical track career path and development program that allows our SMEs to deepen knowledge in their given area, furthering both their career satisfaction and their value. We partner with these SMEs to create scalable, technology-enabled content that can be repurposed for training both employees and customers. This self-paced content can be accessed from our company intranet or customer portal. Assessments are integrated, and employees can earn badges to demonstrate proficiency. These badging programs are also a key element of our internal gig workforce training, the Flex Team, which is deployed around peak business seasons.

Competency Content and Learning Paths

If we are to continue to enhance and grow our people-first culture, it is important to emphasize both the "what" and the "how" in our performance processes and daily interactions. Ultimate's six leadership competencies (big picture orientation, collaboration, creativity and innovation, customer focus, drive for results, and leadership) and our suite of soft skills training programs provide rich content for both self-paced and in-person trainees. Each employee works with their manager to develop a personal development plan that will enhance their capabilities in one to two key competency arenas. Competencies are scaled to match expanding expectations at each successive level in an individual's career. Our learning suite provides mobile-enabled microlearning content in a variety of formats to engage all learning styles.

Personalized Leadership Coaching

We fully integrate personal coaching into all our development programs and the day-to-day interactions of our leaders and their teams. Our team of internal coaches provide structured executive coaching support and follow-up on career development work generated in the LEAD US classes.

Additionally, the coaching team engages with leaders and their people based on opportunities highlighted in our Perception surveys. Perception's verbatim feedback and natural language processing provides a depth of understanding that goes far beyond the survey scores and allows us to create truly customized solutions for these teams.

These initiatives are effective because of the agility, transparency, and openness of our culture. The tone of these engagements is partnership versus reprisal. Our development programs also set clear expectations for our leaders to serve as ever-present coaches to their people. We stress continuous feedback and a regular cadence of development dialogue. The final performance review at year-end should simply be the 365th conversation of the year.

Mentoring

We have several targeted mentoring programs that connect individual contributors and young leaders to senior leadership. These include the Leadership mentoring program, Women in Leadership mentoring program, Women Supporting Women mentoring program (focused on advancing women in our technical organizations), and Technical and Peer mentoring programs. Ultimate also has several vibrant special interest groups that cut across the business to create connections around shared experiences or passions, including UltiVets, PrideUS, Women in Leadership, Women in Technology, and UltiHope for cancer survivors.

■ ■ ■

Role modeling is essential in any learning culture, and leaders must demonstrate their commitment to your organization's culture and values. Success lies in creating and maintaining an adaptive system that continually reinforces the concept that the whole is greater than the sum of its parts. At Ultimate, our culture isn't just something we talk about—it is a living, breathing organism. It links every employee and deepens our connection to them as well as their connection to one another. We see this in the transparency and accessibility of our leaders, who consistently maintain open doors, host dozens of informal events, and work side by side on community volunteer events.

Our people-first leaders are thoughtful and considerate, celebrating birthdays, crowd-funding to help employees in need, and visiting sick or injured employees.

Recently, an Ultimate employee named Molly lost her home to a house fire. This devastating loss thankfully resulted in no loss of human life, but Molly lost all her possessions. Within a day, her fellow employees crowdfunded more than $15,000 in cash to help her buy essentials and restart her life, as well as a new printer and configured laptop. Everyone contributed—not just her team or those who knew Molly, but every top leader and their direct reports. This is an example of culture in action: a groundswell of support from team members, for team members.

At Ultimate, it is easy to find stories of love and generosity because we truly behave like a family. But, in order for this culture to perpetuate, that love and generosity has to be balanced with accountability and business performance. We must have the means to take care of our people at each successive stage of our growth, and that requires business success. Our people, talent, and learning teams hold leaders accountable for the health of their teams and, through our Talent Insights, link team health directly with team performance. Key performance metrics are tracked and reported in parallel to key people metrics such as employee turnover, span of control, performance ratings, survey scores, compensation, and succession pipeline health. All these factors impact current operational performance as well as future preparedness. Metrics are shared openly to encourage peer accountability and open dialogue on opportunities to improve.

Incentives are also designed to reinforce expectations. Our bonus structures consider individual, team, and overall performance, both top and bottom line. Merit increases are competency based, driven out of our year-end performance review. Every employee owns restricted shares in the company, which maintains focus on the big picture. Finally, reward and recognition programs reinforce behaviors consistent with culture or recognize excellence in customer care. These awards are generous and heralded broadly across the company, by leaders, on our intranet, and in our regular newsletters.

Priority 3: Empower the Organization to Perform at Its Best, Today and in the Future

By treating learning as something that happens during one-off events, learning leaders fail to meet ever-changing business needs. Instead, you need to drive a culture of continuous learning within and across your stakeholders. An agile culture necessitates that the learning organization evolve beyond just providing training to prioritizing customer and employee success. This means transforming your learning strategy from a traditional classroom environment, where scaled "build once and deliver to many" is the norm, to a more personalized omni-channel and blended learning approach. Microlearning methodologies can offer shorter, bite-sized targeted training, as well as self-paced options and just-in-time embedded learning experiences. Additionally, social or peer-to-peer learning communities can be game-changing for engagement and enabling sustainable learning opportunities.

Being able to upskill quickly is also crucial. Learning leaders should position their team as in-touch partners with organizational leaders to stay ahead of business, customer, and employee needs and identify functional skills gaps. At Ultimate, we created a functional skills inventory with training content attached to each skill. This intelligence enables us to quickly create learning paths that combine skills, common issues, troubleshooting tips, and overall context based on the learning outcomes desired. As such, we rely on our subject matter experts (SMEs) as an extension of our learning team. They are brought in to contribute, share their knowledge, and validate our content. Additional keys to driving success at Ultimate include the following.

Learning Ambassadors

A true learning culture permeates our business, undergirded by several key strategic programs. Organizational and individual learning agility is mission critical to the future success of our business, which is scaling rapidly, facing many technology changes, and organizing to scale globally. A big part of our learning culture is promoting the sharing of knowledge and continuous learning. The learning team helps promote this behavior, and our goal is to make it an organizational habit to do so. We identify our SMEs and learning ambassadors and guide them toward sharing their expertise through participating as a panelist on a webinar answering Q&As, facilitating a lunch & learn session, validating and contributing content with the learning team, or writing an article to showcase their expertise. This behavior is rewarded, recognized, and embedded in performance goals.

Leveraging Learning to Create an Internal Gig Workforce

We recently had an incredible example of our learning culture in action. During our busiest time of the year, we asked for volunteers inside Ultimate to help with the backlog of work. We had more than 100 volunteers who wanted to learn a new skill and contribute to our company's success. The learning team created a targeted learning path and helped facilitate training our volunteers. Where we normally would have spent time and money to recruit, hire, and train temporary external employees to tackle this backlog, full-time Ultimate employees invested a few hours of their normal work-week to help make a lasting impact on the organization. The results were outstanding. Our people were proud and honored to assist, learned new skills, and received appreciation from their partnering teams. At the end of the project, our senior executives rewarded and recognized the program participants in various ways. It was inspiring to witness.

Rising Stars

Customer care is a pivotal part of our business. As a subscription business, customers' health and retention are one of our most important operational metrics. Our customer support team delivers excellent service and takes a proactive, consultative approach to prepare for whatever challenge our customers present. This team hires new talent throughout the year, year-over-year.

Our learning and talent acquisition teams worked together to design a Rising Stars program to meet these needs. A specialized recruiting team screens candidates nationally for a customer service mindset. We pre-hire them within 12 to 14 weeks, depending on the role, and place them in the care of a Rising Stars program manager. This leader is responsible for teaching the new team members about our culture, mentoring them throughout the process, and creating a strong sense of purpose and belonging. The Rising Star program is now integral to the success of all three divisions of our services organization, accounting for nearly 73 percent of our customer success frontline team. The Rising Stars team partners with Ultimate's leadership team on workforce planning, organizational preparedness, and seasonal peaks in demand. When team members graduate from the program and are placed in their permanent positions, they achieve the highest marks on all key performance indicators (KPIs). Equally important, the role modeling and coaching provided by program managers during training generates employees full of enthusiasm and cultural pride.

Communities and Networks

At Ultimate, we have an online community for customers and employees to engage and connect. Having a strong community program has had a critical impact on our strategic priorities. It provides a channel for us to deepen our relationship with customers by sharing our culture and thought leadership. It gives customers a way to connect with one another and share best practices. It also provides the learning team with a channel to drive learning campaigns for product adoption or to address trending questions. In addition, it promotes knowledge sharing and presents a tremendous opportunity to develop content and address customer needs by monitoring frequent Q&As. This community also monitors the pulse of the customer without having to send a single survey.

Priority 4: Prepare People to Embrace and Thrive in an Agile Environment

The ability to be agile often depends on how well an organization prepares its staff for change. Learning leaders can serve as champions of change initiatives and guide organizational communications by focusing on the needs of their people, both strategically and tactically. We developed several critical communications programs that keep our people informed about what is happening in the business, strategic initiatives, performance, and company celebrations. Adam Rogers, CEO, and Julie Dodd, COO, host a quarterly "State Of" event that moves across our key office locations and is live-cast to all employees. They speak to key business achievements, call out our UltiExcellence winners (a rewards and recognition program where peers nominate colleagues who demonstrate our culture in action), and share the biggest strategic initiatives on the horizon. The communications team also has a biweekly cadence of employee newsletters that celebrates team members, shares stories and upcoming events, and showcases the diversity of our people.

Change management is also a huge focus for Ultimate. Our communications and engagement team develops customized communications strategies around change as well as programs to teach our leaders how to lead their teams through change using adaptive leadership and prosci change management principles.

Operational leaders can easily be consumed by the daily, often transactional, demands of their business. Our people, talent, and learning organization owns key elements of the message and communicates Ultimate's vision to our people. We help the organization understand the urgency of change initiatives and how they will benefit from them.

Talent and learning leaders provide a vision that rallies around a common goal so our people understand why being an agile learner is foundational to Ultimate Software's success. Our mission to put people first internally and externally requires a hyper-focused emphasis on how we lead, manage, work, and serve our customers. We also coach, train, and support our leaders in communicating our overarching vision, as well as additional communications customized to their own piece of the business.

Priority 5: Leverage Analytics to Understand the Workforce Dynamics

A final component to agile learning culture is data and analytics. If learning leaders tapping into whatever talent and human capital analytics are available to make decisions, they are not preparing the organization to respond to employee feedback.

At Ultimate, we use our employee feedback tool to survey employees biannually. By analyzing both qualitative and quantitative data, and distributing a follow-up survey to gauge improvement, we gain a comprehensive understanding of employee experience trends and opportunities. Our survey focuses on five key areas: team health, manager quality, tools and resources, meaningful work, and opportunities for growth and advancement. We also research what our team members value most about working at Ultimate Software and what we can do to improve the company.

We use insights from these surveys to proactively adjust corporate policies and expectations. In 2017, for example, we adopted an Unlimited PTO (UPTO) policy to accommodate employee requests for more flexible schedules. We consider key indicators of employee engagement including turnover (which is currently less than 4 percent), morale, and managerial effectiveness. Open-response questions provide unfiltered, qualitative feedback that is used to improve every aspect of the employee experience.

We also leverage our product suite to provide team-level insights to help our leaders close skills gaps, deepen leadership efficiency, and cultivate young, high-potential leaders with purposeful management of our span of care. Our Team Health Score in our Talent Insights platform allows leaders to quickly identify where they need to focus their attention. This score considers succession pipeline health, retention, engagement in our LEAD US programs, performance management scores, and engagement survey scores. All this insight is combined to provide a comprehensive overview of the teams operating under a leader.

Our learning team also uses data to identify trending customer issues or questions and deploy just-in-time learning solutions to ensure they receive help quickly and efficiently. This has dramatically lowered demands for our customer success teams and positively influenced customer satisfaction. Finally, data-driven insights into customer demand for frontline service people inform our hiring plans for key operationally embedded teams such as the Flex Team and Rising Stars.

Old Habits Die Hard

Inherent in an agile learning culture is the recognition that it is ongoing—one is never finished being agile. By understanding and embracing this challenge with urgency and passion, you can fuel engagement across your organization. Change and growth are hard, but setting a meaningful vision and engaging people in this vision is paramount to organizational success. Every business has two choices: to transform or to enjoy a slow and potentially painful death.

Chief talent and learning officers must actively lead their organizations; this is not a passive role. Here are a few lessons we learned that may help guide you on your journey:

» **The agile organization's people and learning strategy must be considered a business imperative**, not just a set of HR initiatives. At Ultimate, our people, talent, and learning strategy is material to how the organization grows, partners with customers, innovates, and scales globally. Our people-first culture is institutionalized throughout the organization.

» **The chief talent or learning officer position is a game-changing leadership role**, directly responsible and accountable for creating a learning strategy that drives sustained business value. Leaders in this role must lead with strategy and courage, and partner with leaders across the organization. They must also be willing to speak to power about topics related to culture, organizational health, and talent capability.

» **Leadership is not a spectator sport.** Business leaders and frontline managers play an active and engaged role in developing the agile organization. They must be hired, deployed, developed, and rewarded for behaving in ways that align and propagate.

» **People need to come to work as their authentic selves.** This is not just a diversity slogan but rather a true business driver to foster passion, engagement, and true inclusion. Encourage authentic participation in your people and you unlock sustainable and differentiated growth, customer obsession, and true innovation.

Conclusion:
Moving Forward

Tamar Elkeles

So what's next? Through the pages in this book and from the expertise of these forward-focused chief talent and learning officers, we've learned that the path ahead requires us to add value to our organizations differently than we did before. These colleagues have paved the way and we are grateful. While we have made significant progress in expanding our roles and overall organizational impact, much more still needs be done. Now is our time. Uncertainty is driving us all to learn quickly and embrace flexibility. Anyone who isn't learning today will not be relevant tomorrow. Any organization that isn't a learning organization will succumb to disruption.

Innovating, inventing, and adapting are essential for businesses to succeed and grow. That requires a commitment to continuous learning and quickly capitalizing on near-term opportunities. Opportunity motivates experimentation. Risk taking, being uncomfortable with the status quo, questioning—these are the characteristics of tomorrow's chief talent and learning officers.

The past may not have adequately prepared us for "the next." Instead, the future requires us to learn as we go. We need to think differently and be bold. We must embrace the notion that we are business executives first and talent and learning executives second. We don't just occupy a seat at the table—we lead the meeting!

Our agenda is not predetermined. It is fluid and changing just like our companies and our industries. We must take pride in understanding the business innately and use business data to drive our thinking, establish priorities, and determine critical initiatives. Learning is not something we "do." It's embedded into every part of the organization and into everybody's work. We don't just manage learning or talent—we lead the organization!

What we've also learned through our journey is that award-winning learning and talent organizations are continuously embracing new ways of working, new strategies, new technologies, new models, and new perspectives so they can be resilient and agile for the long term. Sometimes the most important insights come from outside our industry, profession, and geography. We must leverage diverse thinking and vital inflection points to elevate our important work and deliver even greater business impact. Organizational change begins with us. Every opportunity to increase organizational productivity and performance is an opportunity to deliver value. We don't just develop talent—we build businesses!

While the collective wisdom and experiences of the chief talent and learning officers who contributed to this book are very different, they all demonstrate that the way to build an award-winning organization is to think, behave, and lead strategically. They are catalysts in developing strategic capabilities across their workforce and within their companies. Independent of their title, functional role, or responsibilities, they leveraged and expanded their field of influence and impact. They didn't wait for an invitation to challenge the status quo. They took the initiative to improve their organizations and deliver business results. They are trailblazers who gave us a road map for how to continuously stay relevant, respected, and valued.

In Peter Senge's groundbreaking 1990 book, *The Fifth Discipline*, he described learning organizations as places "where people continually expand their capacity to create the results they truly desire, where new and expansive patterns of thinking are nurtured, where collective aspiration is set free, and where people are continually learning how to learn together."

Twenty years later we are doing that and so much more. Here's to the next 20 years and continuing to learn together.

References

Anthony, S., S. Viguerie, E. Schwartz, and J. Van Landeghem. 2018. "Corporate Longevity Forecast: Creative Destruction Is Accelerating." Innosight. innosight.com/insight/creative-destruction.

Association for Talent Development (ATD) and Institute for Corporate Productivity (i4cp). 2015. *Leaders as Teachers: Engaging Employees in High-Performance Learning.* Alexandria, VA: ATD Press.

Association for Talent Development (ATD). 2019. *2019 State of the Industry.* Alexandria, VA: ATD Press.

Bersin, J. 2018. "The Learning Experience Platform (LXP) Market Expands." September 27. joshbersin.com/2018/09/the-learning-experience-platform-lxp -market-expands.

Betof, E. 2009. *Leaders as Teachers: Unlock the Teaching Potential of Your Company's Best and Brightest.* San Francisco: Berrett-Koehler.

Church, E., S. Lambin, and L. Yu. 2012. "15th Annual Global CEO Survey." PwC. pwc.com/gx/en/ceo-survey/pdf/15th-global-pwc-ceo-survey.pdf.

Enron Corp. 2001. *Enron Annual Report, 2000.* Houston, TX: Enron.

Galbraith, J.R. "The STAR Model." jaygalbraith.com/images/pdfs/StarModel.pdf.

George, B., and D. Baker. 2011. *True North Groups; A Powerful Path to Personal and Leadership Development.* San Francisco: Berrett-Koehler.

Gino, F. 2018. "Why Curiosity Matters." *Harvard Business Review,* September–October.

Gladwell, M. 2002. "The Talent Myth." *The New Yorker,* July 22.

Google. n.d. "Our Approach to Search." google.com/search/howsearchworks/mission

Inc. Staff. n.d. "Corporate Culture." Inc.com Encyclopedia. inc.com/encyclopedia /corporate-culture.html.

Knoll, A., H. Otani, R. Skeel, and K. Van Horn. 2017. "Learning Style, Judgements of Learning, and Learning of Verbal and Visual Information." *British Journal of Psychology* 108(3): 544–563.

Lovell Corporation. 2017. "The Change Generation." lovellcorporation.com /the-change-generation-report.

Lucas Jr., H.C., and J.M. Goh. 2009. "Disruptive technology: How Kodak Missed the Digital Photography Revolution." *The Journal of Strategic Information Systems* 18(1): 46–55.

McCall, M., M. Lombardo, and A. Morrison. 1988. *Lessons of Experience: How Successful Executives Develop on the Job.* New York: Free Press.

McCall Jr., M.W. 1998. "High Flyers, Developing the Next Generation of Leaders." *Harvard Business Review.*

Neal, A. 2013. *Leading From the Edge: Global Executives Share Strategies for Success*. Alexandria, VA: ASTD Press.

NikeU. 2012. "NikeU Trailer." youtu.be/rjKT0HWU11M.

Partners in Leadership. "The Results Pyramid." partnersinleadership.com /insights-publications/tag/the-results-pyramid.

Ray, C. n.d. "Aligning Brand, Purpose, and Culture." Interbrand. interbrand.com /views/grow-on-purpose-aligning-brand-purpose-and-culture.

Red Hat. 2019a. "IBM Closes Landmark Acquisition of Red Hat for $34 Billion; Defines Open, Hybrid Cloud Future." Press Release, July 9. redhat.com /en/about/press-releases/ibm-closes-landmark-acquisition-red-hat-34-billion -defines-open-hybrid-cloud-future.

Red Hat. 2019b. "The Book of Red Hat: Our Shared History, Purpose, and Culture." Raleigh, NC: Red Hat.

Rigoni, B., and B. Nelson. 2016. "Few Millennials Are Engaged at Work." *Gallup Business Journal*. news.gallup.com/businessjournal/195209/few-millennials -engaged-work.aspx.

Rogers, E.M. 1971. *Diffusion of Innovations*, 3rd ed. New York: Free Press.

Rogowsky, B., B. Calhoun, and P. Tallal. 2015. "Matching Learning Style to Instructional Method: Effects on Comprehension." *Journal of Educational Psychology* 107(1): 64–78.

Senge, P. 1990. *The Fifth Discipline: The Art & Practice of the Learning Organization*. New York: Doubleday.

Sinek, S. 2009. *Start With Why: How Great Leaders Inspire Everyone to Take Action*. Penguin: New York.

Smith, J. (Speaker), and M. Theodotou (Producer). 2019. "Collective Curiosity." [TED Talk]. TEDxDAU. Internal Event, June 12.

Startup Genome. 2019. "Global Startup Ecosystem Report 2019." startupgenome.com/reports.

Thomson, L., L. Lu, and D. Pate. 2017. "2017 Workplace Learning Report: How Modern Learning and Development Pros Are Tackling Top Challenges." LinkedIn Learning Solutions.

Udemy. 2018. "Udemy in Depth: 2018 Millennials at Work Report." Udemy. research.udemy.com/wp-content/uploads/2018/06/Udemy_2018_Measuring _Millennials_Report_20180618.pdf.

Vark-Learn Limited. 2019. "The Vark Questionnaire (Version 8.01)." vark-learn.com/wp-content/uploads/2014/08/The-VARK-Questionnaire.pdf.

Watershed. 2019. "Caterpillar xAPI Case Study." watershedlrs.com/caterpillar -xapi-case-study.

World Economic Forum. 2019. *The Future of Jobs Report*. weforum.org/reports.

About the Contributors

Ruth Almen, leadership and executive services director, leads the team responsible for identifying and developing the next generation of senior leaders to be ready to deliver on the company's future business strategy. From enterprise executive talent planning to designing differentiated leadership experiences and development journeys for global leaders, she is focused on maximizing scale, impact, and reach with innovative solutions to prepare a pipeline of executive leaders with the skills and mindsets needed for the future. Ruth has spent more than 15 years expanding and deepening her expertise in leadership development and learning across a variety of large, global companies. In her most recent role as head of global leadership development for 3M, Ruth led a global team responsible for high-potential leadership development for top executives to frontline leaders. Ruth holds both a BS and MS in human resource development from the University of Minnesota.

Michelle Braden is passionate about learning and development—and about using her business savvy and leadership expertise to look beyond typical adult learning strategies and toward innovative talent development approaches that drive true business impact. She is laser-focused on enabling WEX team members to grow as individuals and professionals in their careers while delivering upon business goals and providing world-class services and solutions in the financial technology industry.

Michelle recently left TELUS International after serving as chief learning officer and vice president of global learning excellence for six and a half years. There, along with her globally based team, Michelle built a multi-award-winning learning strategy that fundamentally changed how the organization built and maintained a robust leadership pipeline while providing team members with a comprehensive learning journey. During her tenure at TELUS International, she was featured in the November 2018 issue of *Chief Learning Officer* magazine.

With 25 years of successful management experience in and around leadership and talent development, instructional design and development, information technology, and sales domains, Michelle understands the impact that proficient and fulfilled employees have on engagement, attrition, and business performance. She has an MBA with a leadership specialty and a BA in management/communication with a minor in information technology.

Susan Burnett has dedicated the last 37 years of her career catalyzing the strategic changes and capabilities required to grow and transform individuals and organizations. She has held executive positions at Hewlett Packard, Gap, Deloitte, Yahoo!, and BTS, where she led business transformation and restructuring, global marketing services, cultural renewal, leadership development at all levels, succession, diversity, and employee engagement.

Susan is chair of the board of directors for Rising International. Previously, she led the strategic directions committee for the Association for Talent Development (ATD), was a member of the board of directors, and chaired the board for two years.

Susan is currently CEO of DYL Consulting, an organization that brings Designing Your Life workshops to the public and to corporations that are re-imagining career development and employee engagement. She is a regular speaker and author on Designing Your Life, talent management, and leadership development.

Laura Lee Gentry is senior vice president of employee experience with Ultimate Software. She believes that excellence in talent management is the key to driving a differentiated, sustainable competitive advantage and brings her more than 30 years of experience as a business leader, global strategist, and talent consultant to help create an agile, scalable, and thriving organization.

Gale Halsey is currently the vice president of human resources for Ford Motor Credit Company. Prior to that role, she was the chief learning officer for Ford Motor Company, where she was responsible for developing and implementing the vision, strategy, and global organization structure for all OD and learning activities across Ford. She coordinated the activities of the 10 functional learning and development organizations, global leadership development programs, onboarding, and coaching strategies. Gale's team also owned functional competency framework deployment standards. She was responsible for the business operations of the Ford Training and Development Center, the Organization Development Institute, L&OD IT platforms, and university partnership programs.

Gale has held a number of positions within Ford, including director of human resources for Ford of Mexico, and director of negotiations planning and global labor strategy, since joining in 1994. Gale also worked for the Pepsi Bottling Company for two years as a regional human resource manager. She has a master's degree in labor and industrial relations from Michigan State University.

Chris Holmes is the head of learning at Amazon Web Services (AWS) Professional Services. Formerly the functional learning director at Booz Allen Hamilton, he led that organization's functional development and learning operations and designed learning models and experiences that developed technical skills against current and emerging business demands. Chris has more than 20 years of experience in corporate human capital, driving business transformation and results through communications, change, culture, and learning initiatives. She's managed execution of full-scale program oversight from analysis to implementation, has leveraged human capital practices to measure and improve workforce productivity, and has supported enterprise performance improvement. Chris has also supported broad talent management efforts including leadership competency framework development, change initiatives, and talent assessment. She holds a BA in English education from the University of West Florida, an Executive Leadership Certificate from Cornell University, and is certified in Human Capital Strategist, Hogan Assessments, and Kirkpatrick.

Jayne Johnson has dedicated the better part of her career to leadership and organization development. Currently, she is vice president of enterprise learning and development at Alkermes. She has worked for global organizations from GE and Deloitte to CPG firms and life sciences. Joining GE as a computer programmer right out of college, she transitioned from IT to HR and never looked back. She held several L&OD roles while at GE, the last six years of which were at GE's John F. Welch Leadership Centre, also known as Crotonville. While there, she was responsible for GE's leadership development curriculum and the customer education team, providing strategic consultative services and training to GE's customers. She later held similar roles at Deloitte, Keurig Green Mountain, and a couple of biotech companies in the Boston area.

Jayne has been a member of a few boards, enjoys mentoring for Women Unlimited, and had the pleasure of serving as a Girl Scout troop leader for her daughter and manager of the local Little League group for her son.

Andrew Kilshaw is the vice president of organizational development and learning for Shell's Downstream business. He and his global team of more than 200 people are tasked with building future-proof capabilities for Shell's manufacturing, chemicals, trading and marketing teams, and guiding a seismic organizational and cultural transformation to lead and thrive through the energy transition. Prior to Shell, Andrew was VP HR–Asia-Pacific & Latin America at Nike, the world's leading supplier of athletic footwear, apparel, and equipment. During his nine years at the company, Andrew held several other diverse roles with a focus on helping organizations and people realize their full potential. Upon joining Nike in 2010, Andrew assumed the newly created position of chief learning officer. In this role, he and his team were responsible for creating a global learning function and deploying leadership, management, and functional development to Nike employees around the world. Subsequently, Andrew also acted as the HR leader for the global marketing functions, the Jordan brand (where he also led the strategy team) as well as Nike's business-transforming digital function. Before joining Nike, he held talent management and organization development leadership roles at BlackRock, the world's largest asset manager. His prior experience spans several industries, functions, and geographies, having additionally lived in France, Switzerland (where he received an MBA with a distinction in leadership from IMD), and his native UK. Andrew holds a master's in physics and French from the University of Manchester (UK) and Université Paul Sabatier, Toulouse (France).

Aimee George Leary, global talent officer, leads Booz Allen Hamilton's strategy and execution of a comprehensive employee value proposition, which creates a shared culture and engaging work environment and helps enable rewarding professional experiences. She is responsible for building talent programs that create a strong, diverse talent pipeline and empower all talent through skill development, career opportunity and choice, and comprehensive reward and wellness programs. Aimee's key areas of expertise include talent strategy, HR operations, change management, communications, employee engagement, and building a culture of innovation. She holds a BS in communications media from Indiana University of Pennsylvania and an MS in instructional technology from Bloomsburg University of Pennsylvania.

Annmarie Neal is Ultimate Software's chief human resources officer. She is also a partner and the chief talent officer with Hellman & Friedman, where she specializes in business value creation and transformation through leadership and organizational excellence. She brings more than 25 years of global experience consulting with business executives and senior leaders across a range of industries to her writing, speaking engagements, business management, and consultation. She also published *Leading From the Edge* in 2013 with ATD Press.

Brad Samargya is the global chief learning officer for KPMG, responsible for overall learning and development for KPMG's 200,000-plus professionals across more than 150 member firms. Prior to KPMG, he held several senior leadership positions, including chief learning officer for Ericsson and CA Technologies, group VP and global head of learning for Siebel Systems/Oracle, and both VP of education and CFO of Sybase Professional Services. Brad started his career as a senior manager at Price Waterhouse and is also a former CPA. He has significant experience as a transformational leader building global learning and consulting teams tasked with driving business transformations in software, services, and technology for employees, customers, and channel partners. Brad is a frequent keynote speaker, his organizations have won numerous learning awards for best-in-class programs, and he was a Nobel Future of Learning Panelist.

Martha Soehren was with Comcast Cable since 2000 before she retired in 2020 as the chief talent development officer and SVP of Comcast University. She also is a founding member of ATD's CTDO Next, a network of the world's top talent development executives who are shaping what's next in talent. She can be reached at martha_soehren@comcast.com.

Marina Theodotou is the center director for operations and analytics in workflow learning directorate at the Defense Acquisition University. She holds a doctorate in education specializing in organizational change and leadership from the Rossier School of Education at the University of Southern California.

Kevin D. Wilde serves as an Executive Leadership Fellow at the School of Management, University of Minnesota, where he teaches executive MBA leadership courses and researches leadership development and coachability. He is the author of the *Coachability Practices Assessment (CPR)* and his work can be found at thecoachableleader.com.

Kevin's 34-year corporate career at General Electric and General Mills primarily involved talent managing and development, including serving as the global chief learning officer for General Mills. The organization received numerous awards for innovative development programs, including a *Fortune* magazine top ranking as one of the best firms for leadership development. *CLO* magazine recognized Kevin as CLO of the year in 2007 and the number 1 learning elite organization. He continues to contribute to the field of talent and leadership development through speaking, writing, and advising. His greatest delight is mentoring the next generation of innovative talent development leaders.

Index

In this index, *f* denotes figure and *t* denotes table.

A

accreditation, 49
action learning, 91
activation phase (learning ecosystem), 45–46, 45*f*
ADDIE model, 71, 76, 78, 109
adoption phase (learning ecosystem), 45*f*, 46–47
Agile approach
    about, 131–132
    analytics, 141–142
    business imperatives, 133–142
    change, preparing for, 140–141
    culture fit, 134–135
    empowering organization, 138–140
    leader characteristics, 132–133
    leader development, 135–138
    learning capabilities, matching with business capabilities, 76–78
    lessons learned, 142–143
    organizational culture, 132
AIDAR model, 37, 37*f*, 38*t*
Airbnb, 39
alignment to business. *See* business alignment
Amazon, 38, 39
Aristotle, 84
authentic selves, 143
awards, ix–x, 50, 74

B

Baker, Doug, 92
BBC, 58–59, 62
BD (Becton, Dickinson), 58
benchmarking, 49
Betof, Ed, 58, 83
BlackRock, 36, 37

Blight, Garretson, 124
Booz Allen
    Collaborative Learning Framework, 120–122, 121*f*, 129–130
    Community Leadership Project, 126
    hackathons and capture the flag events, 123–124
    Leadership Excellence Program, 125–126
    Learning Circles, 127
    Summer Games, 124–125
    Tech Excellence, 122–123
Bowerman, Bill, 36
Brain Candy, 64
brand, learning, 36–37, 37*f*, 38*t*
budget. *See also* efficiency and effectiveness
    company-wide initiatives, 19
    cuts to, 1
    minding, 99–100
    plans to back up, 5
    shared services, 20–21
    talent and organization development, 18
    unit, 19
business acumen, 73, 96
business alignment
    budget, using plans to back up, 5
    engagement, 6–7
    litmus test, 7
    staff capability, building, 2–3
    strategic learning business plan, 3–4
    structure and processes for, 15–21
business engagement, 6–7
business imperatives, 142
business metrics, 23–24, 24*t*, 107, 108, 108*f*
business needs, assessing, 72–73
Business Partner Planner, 67

business-first mindset and skill set, 56–59

C

capture the flag events, 123–124

Casterline, Jonathon, 79

Caterpillar, 51–52, 56, 62

certification process, 97

change, preparing for, 140–141

chief executive officers (CEOs), 41, 51, 52

chief financial officers (CFOs), 5

chief learning officers (CLOs), 30–31, 142

coaching, 92, 137

collaborative learning
  about, 119–120
  achieving, 128
  Collaborative Learning Framework, 120–122, 121f, 129–130
  Community Leadership Project, 126
  hackathons and capture the flag events, 123–124
  Leadership Excellence Program, 125–126
  Learning Circles, 127
  Summer Games, 124–125
  Tech Excellence, 122–123

Collaborative Learning Framework, 120–122, 121f, 129–130

Comcast Cable, 110–111, 114, 115f, 116–118, 117f

communications, 48, 50–51, 90–91, 99, 140–141

community, 140

Community Leadership Project, 126

company longevity, 41

company-wide initiatives, 19

Compaq, 22–23

competence gaps, 3–4

competency content and learning paths, 136–137

connections, fostering, 129

content, as learning ecosystem building block, 44

continuous improvement, 49–50

corporate culture. See organizational culture

Covert-Weiss, Sheila, 77–78, 80

COVID-19 epidemic, v, vi

critics of learning strategy, 104

Crotonville, 84, 85, 91

culture. See learning culture; organizational culture

customer, understanding, 75–76

D

data. See also metrics
  collecting right, 49, 51
  as learning ecosystem building block, 44
  skills, 109–110

data analytics, 110–111, 141–142

decision making, 17, 62–63

DeFilippo, Dave, 85

Deloitte
  decision making, 17
  dual reporting, 16
  financial planning and reporting, 18, 19
  leaders as teachers, 92
  mission, 14–15

doctor–patient analogy, 3

document development, 114

Drucker, Peter, 24

dual reporting, 16

E

Eastman Kodak, 42

Ebbinghaus forgetting curve, 86

efficiency and effectiveness
  about, 95–96, 104–105
  business, knowing, 96
  critics of learning strategy, 104
  evaluating, 102–103
  learning team development, 98–99, 103–104
  measuring, 112, 113f
  momentum, continuing, 104
  prioritizing efforts, 96–97
  simplicity and, 97–98
  solutions, marketing, 102
  technology, leveraging, 100–101

Elkeles, Tamar, 59, 60, 61

email, 91
employee engagement, 42–43, 107, 108*f*, 122
employee surveys, 141–142
empowering organization, 138–140
engagement, 6–7, 42–43, 107, 108*f*, 122
Evans, Tom, 66
experience, learning through, 34, 34*t*

F
"faculty within" thinking, 63
Fedora, 51
feedback, 6–7, 39–40
financial planning and reporting, 17–21
fireside chats, 92
Fleming, Neil, 36
formal learning
    culture and, 35, 35*t*
    as term, 111
Freidman, Greg, 91

G
Galbraith, Jay, 11, 11*f*, 13, 13*f*
Gap, 15–16, 17, 24*t*
General Electric (GE), 84, 85, 91, 92
General Mills, 55–56
Generation Z, 30
George, Bill, 92
gig workforce, internal, 139
Golden State Warriors, 21–22
Google, 33
governance, 44–45, 62–63, 114, 115*f*

H
hackathons, 123–124
Hagberg Consulting Group, 33
Hewlett-Packard (HP)
    Compaq, merger with, 22–23
    dual reporting, 16
    financial planning and reporting, 18, 19, 20–21
    as learning organization, 12–14, 13*f*
    metrics, 24*t*
    peer knowledge sharing platform, 64
hiring, 48, 134–135
Hudson-Martin, Gerry, 61

human-centered design, 75–76

I
IMD, 30
impact
    business metrics, 107, 108, 108*f*
    data skills, 109–110
    employee engagement metrics, 107, 108*f*
    future trends, 118
    governance model, 114, 115*f*
    impact (ROI) story, 115–118, 115*f*, 117*f*
    individual, 113
    measuring what matters, 112
    metrics, making meaning of, 113–114
    quality and efficiency of talent development, 112, 113*f*
    talent development metrics, 107, 108*f*
    workplace transformations, 110–113, 113*f*
improvement, continuous, 49–50
incentives, 138
inclusive team construct, 130
individual impact, 113
infrastructure, enabling, 120
initiatives, company-wide, 19
innovation, 43
integration phase (learning ecosystem), 45*f*, 47
Interbrand, 40
internships, 124–125

J
Jordan, Mike, 64

K
Kerr, Steve, 21–22
Keurig Green Mountain, 88
Kippen, Kimo, 55, 58, 59–60, 61
Kodak, 42

L
Lauber, Rob, 74, 80–81
LEAD US series, 135–136

leaders
  benefits of leaders as teachers to, 84–85, 100
  characteristics of Agile, 132–133
  communications, 90–91, 99
  developing, 97, 135–138
leaders as teachers (LAT)
  about, 83
  benefits to L&D function, 86–87
  benefits to leader, 84–85, 100
  benefits to learner, 85–86
  benefits to organization, 84, 100
  deploying, 89–92, 90*f*
  preparing leaders for role as, 88–89
  selecting leaders for, 87–88
  strategies, 69
leadership coaching, 137
Leadership Excellence Program, 125–126
Leading from the Edge (Neal), 132–133
Learn & Grow portfolio, 99, 101
learning ambassadors, 139
learning brand, 36–37, 37*f,* 38*t*
learning capabilities
  business capabilities and, 75–80
  learning team's, 73–74
Learning Circles, 127
learning culture
  formal learning, 35, 35*t*
  learning ecosystem and, 47–50
  learning from others, 34, 35*t*
  learning through experience, 34, 34*t*
learning ecosystem
  about, 42
  activation phase, 45–46, 45*f*
  adoption phase, 45*f,* 46–47
  building blocks, 43–45
  culture of learning as oxygen for, 47–50
  importance of, 42–43
  integration phase, 45*f,* 47
  journey, charting, 52
  life cycle phases, 45–47, 45*f*
  use cases, 50–52

learning experience platform (LXP), 44, 101
learning from others, 34, 35*t*
learning management system (LMS), 20, 100
learning organizations
  business alignment, 15–21
  culture, 24–27, 25*f,* 26*f*
  home, starting transformation at, 9–10
  metrics, 23–24, 24*t*
  mission, 14–15
  people, 21–23
  systems mindset, 11–14, 11*f,* 13*f*
learning purpose, 31–32
learning strategy, 96–98, 104. *See also* business alignment
learning styles, 36
learning teams
  about, 71–72
  award-winning, 74
  business acumen, 73
  business needs, assessing, 72–73
  confidence, creativity, and commitment, 48
  developing, 79–80, 98–99, 103–104
  learning capabilities, matching with business capabilities, 75–80
  learning capability, 73–74
  skills, assessing, 73–74
  vendors, external, 80–82
learning through experience, 34, 34*t*
Learning@TI Roadmap, 98, 104
life cycle phases (learning ecosystem), 45–47, 45*f*
linking back to purpose, v–vi
longevity, company, 41
Lovell Corporation, 30

M

management support
  about, 53–54
  business-first mindset and skill set, 56–59
  job aids, 67–69
  partner relationships, 54–56

performance consulting, 59–62
share-to-gain strategies, 62–65
shark, thinking and acting like,
  65–66
strategic learning plans, 4
Marriott International, 61
McKinsey & Company, 56
measurement data. *See* impact; metrics
memory, 86
mentoring, 89–90, 90*f*, 137
metrics
  business, 23–24, 24*t*, 107, 108, 108*f*
  CEO agenda and, 49
  employee engagement, 107, 108*f*
  learning organizations, designing
    effective, 23–24, 24*t*
  making meaning of, 113–114
  organizational culture, 113–114
  talent development, 107, 108*f*
Millennials, 32, 83
mission, 14–15, 98
momentum, continuing, 104
moving forward, 145–146

N
Neal, Annmarie, 132–133
networks, 140
"new normal," v–vii
Nike, 31–32, 33, 36–37, 37*f*, 38, 38*t*, 39

O
Oakes, Kevin, 63
onboarding, 135
open learning landscape, 111
organizational culture
  about, 32–33
  Agile organizations, 132
  formal learning and, 35, 35*t*
  importance of, 24–27, 25*f*, 26*f*
  learning culture, creating
    supporting, 33–36, 34*t*, 35*t*
  learning from others and, 34, 35*t*
  learning through experience and,
    34, 34*t*
  metrics, 113–114
  protecting, 134–135

P
Paine, Nigel, 58–59, 62
Paraxel, 91
partner relationships, 54–56
patterns, finding, 114
peer coaching, 92
peer-to-peer learning, 63–64
people
  as learning ecosystem building
    block, 43–44
  in learning organizations, 21–23
  as theme of book, xii–xiii
performance consulting, 3, 4, 59–62
performance improvement, 43,
  138–140
personal skin in the game, 129
personalization, 38–39, 137
podcasts, 90
priorities, 30, 96–97
problem solving, 48, 51, 120, 123, 129
process, as theme of book, xiii–xv
purpose, v–vi, 31–32

Q
Qualcomm, 60, 61

R
Rapid Content Development, 77–78
recognition, ix
Red Hat, 50–51
resilience, v
reskilling costs, 43
Results Pyramid, 25, 25*f*, 26–27, 26*f*
Ring, 55
Rising Stars program, 140
risks, acknowledging, 66
role modeling, 137–138
Rowley, Dawn, 72–73

S
SAP, 102
Sasson, Steven, 42
Senge, Peter, 146
70-20-10 framework, 34–35, 34*t*, 35*t*
shared services, 20–21
share-to-gain strategies, 62–65

Shark Tank, 53, 54, 55, 65. *See also*
    management support
Sinek, Simon, 31, 48
skills, assessing, 73–74
Smith, Josh, 43
sponsorship, 17
staff capability, building, 2–3
Star Model, 11, 11*f*, 13, 13*f*
Stedham, Adam, 61
strategic plan, 3–4, 49, 51–52
Strategies for Leaders as Teachers, 69
strategy to competence, 3–4
Summer Games, 124–125
surveys, employee, 141–142
swag and giveaways, 102
swearing, 25
systems mindset, 11–14, 11*f*, 13*f*

T

Tactical Advancements for the Next
    Generation (TANG), 43
talent development metrics, 107, 108*f*
Tech Excellence, 122–123
TechieTalks, 79
technical career path and development, 136
technology, 44, 78–79, 100–101
TELUS International, 96–97, 98–100,
    101, 102, 103–104
translation needs, 82
troubleshooting skills, 116–117, 117*f*
True North groups, 92

U

Ultimate Software
    about, 133–134
    analytics, 141–142
    change, preparing for, 140–141
    culture fit, 134–135
    empowering organization,
        138–140
    leader development, 135–138
unit budgets, 19

V

value proposition, 111
Value-Add Analysis, 68
Van Dam, Nick, 56
Vance, David, 56, 60, 62
VARK model, 36
vendors, external, 80–82
videos, 90–91, 99, 102
virtual, going, vi
VISA, 55
vision, x–xii, 98

W

"why," starting with, 48, 50
Willyerd, Karie, 55
work value priorities, 30
workplace transformations, 110–113, 113*f*

Y

Yahoo!, 14, 16, 18, 26, 26*f*
Young, Bo, 50

About the Editor

Tamar Elkeles, Ph.D.

Tamar is an experienced Human Resources Executive, Chief Learning Officer (CLO) and thought leader in the talent, learning and organizational development field. She has expertise managing global growth and leading international teams, as well as an extensive background implementing best in class people practices in technology companies. Tamar is currently the Head of Human Resources for XCOM Labs, a wireless technology company propelling the next mobile revolution. Prior to this role she was Chief Talent Executive for Atlantic Bridge Capital, a global venture capital firm focused on technology investments. Previously Tamar was the Chief People Officer for Quixey, a Silicon Valley tech start-up, and before that was the CLO at Qualcomm. In her nearly 25 year tenure as CLO at Qualcomm she helped grow the company into one of the most successful companies in the world. There she led the development of Qualcomm's workforce, scaling the employee base from 700 to over 31,000 employees worldwide.

She has been featured in several publications including *CLO* Magazine, *Training* Magazine, *T&D* Magazine and *HR* Executive magazine for her leadership and innovative contributions. Throughout her career she has earned numerous awards, including the "Learning Elite Trailblazer" Award (2014), the prestigious "San Diego Women Who Mean Business" Award (1998) and the "Tribute to Women in Industry" Award (2004). In 2010 she was named "CLO of the Year" by CLO Magazine and in 2014 was named "Top Influential" by the *San Diego Daily Transcript* for her significant impact and leadership in the technology industry. In addition to her executive roles, she has authored three books: *The Chief Learning Officer, Measuring the Success of Learning Through Technology* and *The Chief Talent Officer*.

Tamar is a member of the Board of Directors for GP Strategies (NYSE: GPX) as well as a Board Member for The Forbes School of Business & Technology. She also serves on the CLO Magazine Editorial Board and the Association for Talent Development (ATD) Chief Talent Development Officer (CTDO) Next Board. Tamar was a member of The Conference Board's Executive Council on Talent and Organizational Development and also served on the Board of Directors for ATD, the world's premier professional association and leading resource on workplace learning and performance. Tamar holds both a M.S. and a Ph.D. in Organizational Psychology.